A KID'S GUIDE TO
ANIME & MANGA

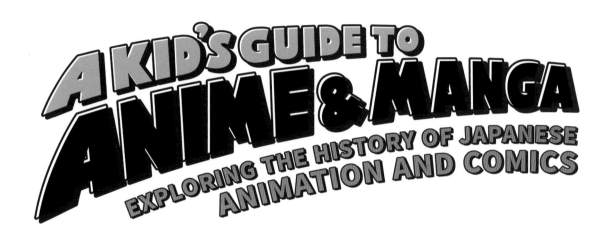

A KID'S GUIDE TO ANIME & MANGA

EXPLORING THE HISTORY OF JAPANESE ANIMATION AND COMICS

SAMUEL SATTIN AND PATRICK MACIAS

ILLUSTRATED BY UTOMARU

RP|KIDS
PHILADELPHIA

Running Press Kids
Hachette Book Group
1290 Avenue of the Americas, New York, NY 10104
www.runningpress.com/rpkids
@runningpresskids

Distributed in the United Kingdom by Little, Brown Book Group UK,
Carmelite House, 50 Victoria Embankment, London, EC4Y 0DZ

Printed in China

First Edition: November 2023

Published by Running Press Kids, an imprint of Perseus Books, LLC, a subsidiary of Hachette Book Group, Inc.
The Running Press Kids name and logo are trademarks of the Hachette Book Group.

The Hachette Speakers Bureau provides a wide range of authors for speaking events. To find out more,
go to www.hachettespeakersbureau.com or email HachetteSpeakers@hbgusa.com.

Running Press books may be purchased in bulk for business, educational, or
promotional use. For more information, please contact your local bookseller or the
Hachette Book Group Special Markets Department at Special.Markets@hbgusa.com.

The publisher is not responsible for websites (or their content) that are not owned by the publisher.

Print book cover and interior design by Mary Boyer.

Library of Congress Cataloging-in-Publication Data
Names: Sattin, Samuel, author. | Macias, Patrick, 1972– author. | Utomaru (Freelance illustrator), illustrator.
Title: A kid's guide to anime & manga : exploring the history of Japanese animation and comics / Samuel Sattin and
Patrick Macias ; illustrated by Utomaru.
Description: First edition. | New York, NY : Running Press Kids, 2023. |
Includes bibliographical references.
Identifiers: LCCN 2022061085 | ISBN 9780762483938 (paperback) | ISBN
9780762483945 (ebook)
Subjects: LCSH: Animated films—Japan—Juvenile literature. | Animated television programs—Japan—Juvenile
literature. | Manga (Comic books)—Juvenile literature. | Comic books, strips, etc.—Japan—Juvenile literature.
Classification: LCC NC1766.J3 S38 2023 | DDC
791.43/340952—dc23/eng/20221227
LC record available at https://lccn.loc.gov/2022061085

ISBNs: 978-0-7624-8393-8 (paperback), 978-0-7624-8394-5 (ebook)

1010

10 9 8 7 6 5 4 3 2

CONTENTS

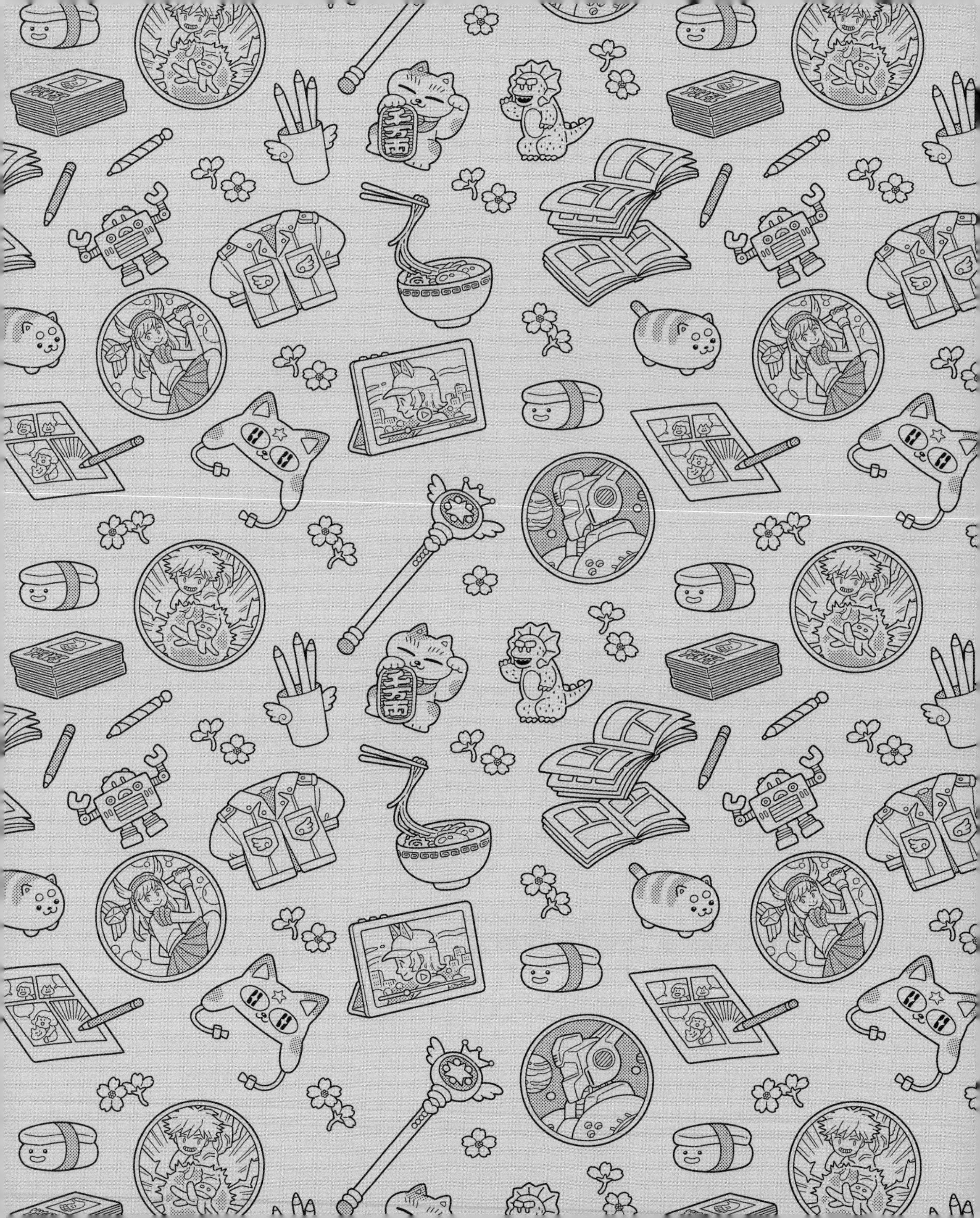

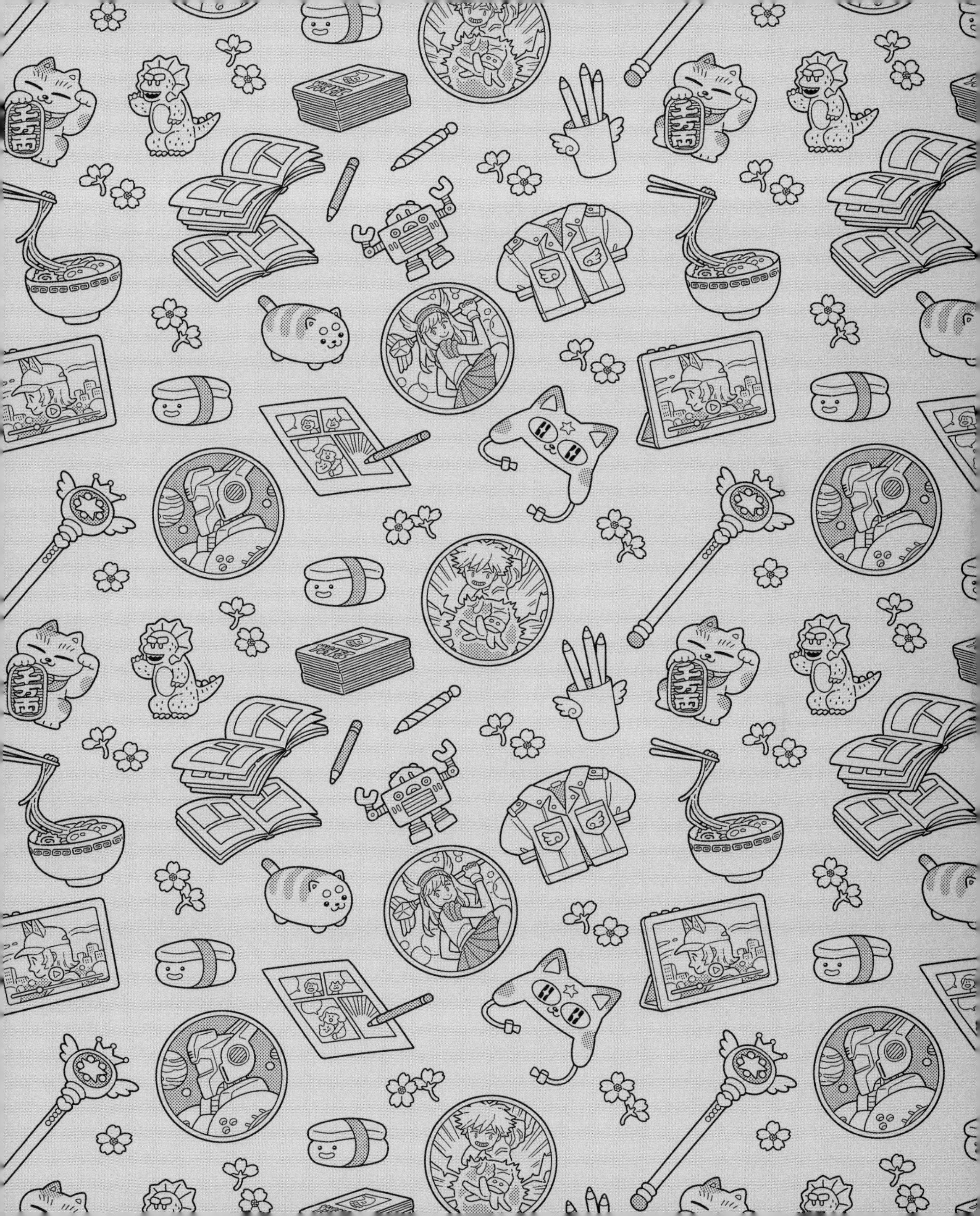

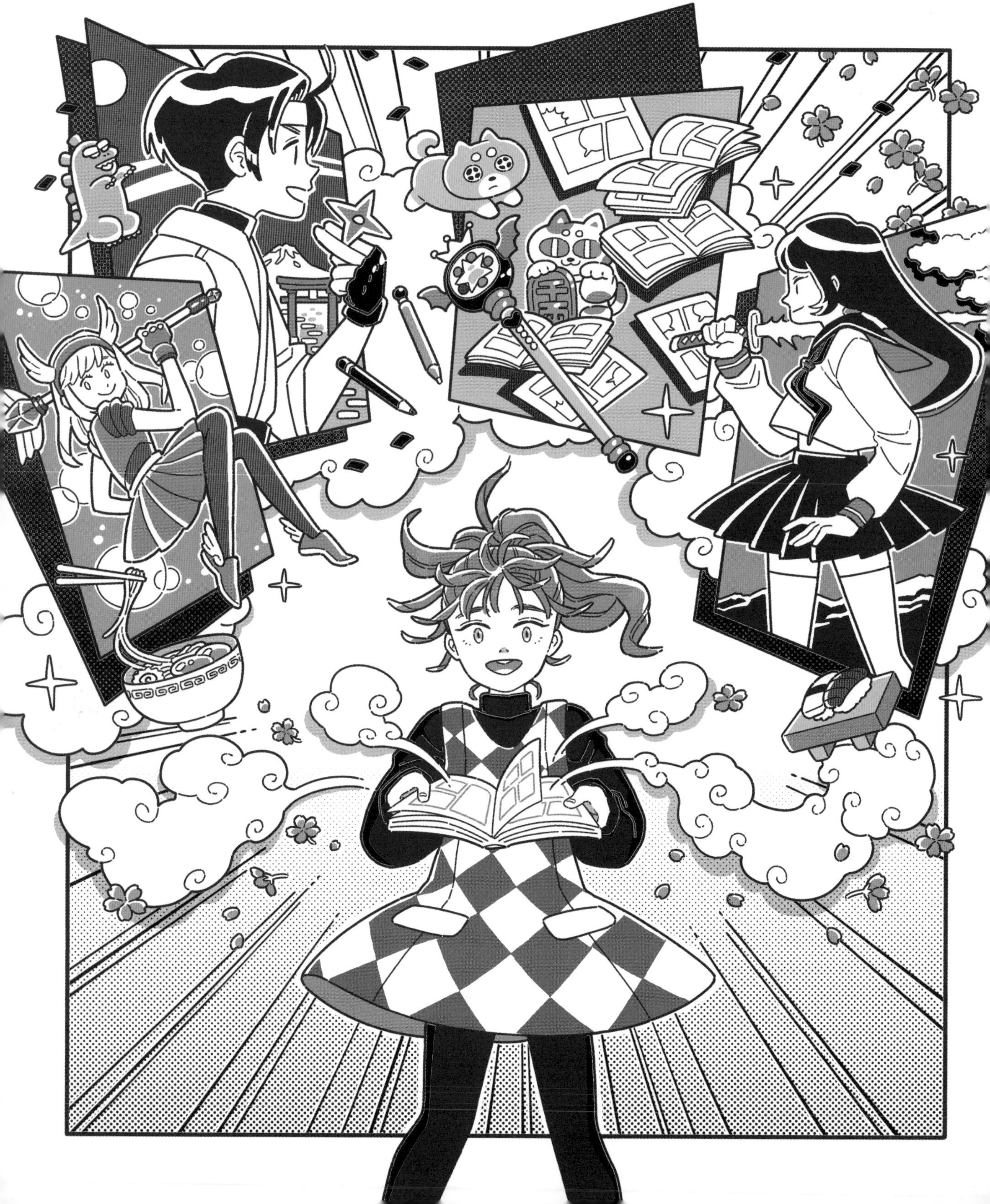

INTRODUCTION

WHEN DID YOU FIRST REALIZE that you like **anime** and **manga**? Were you at a friend's house when someone suggested watching an episode of *Yu-Gi-Oh!* or *Little Witch Academia*? Did one of your parents bring you a volume of *Yotsuba&!* or take you to see a Studio Ghibli film? Or did you start collecting Pokémon cards, begin watching the series, and then fall down the rabbit hole of other ways you could feed your interest? As we write this book, we have our own clear memories of how we discovered anime and manga, at a time when both were a bit harder to find in the United States. We know how special the moment can be when you first enter this new and exciting world.

We're also delighted that, at this moment in time, it's never been easier to get involved with anime and manga. Both have risen to the top of the entertainment world, with manga outselling most comics in the United States and abroad and anime not just rocketing to the top of the movie box office but also taking up huge chunks of what we stream on television. All of this creates near-endless opportunities for **fandom** to thrive.

But with all that popularity and excitement around anime and manga, you might find it a little more daunting to figure out how to get involved in either or both. With so much anime and manga material to choose from, how do you know where to start? Where did all this stuff begin, anyway? Also, how do you make more connections with a larger community that celebrates these stories and characters? These are all questions that we'll be helping you answer in this handy guide. Whether you're just looking for some manga recommendations, industry information, or an introduction to Japanese pop culture, we think you'll come across something here you didn't know about before. And that, **kohai,** is exciting.

Join us as we open the doors to the gigantic world of anime and manga, where amazing new stories, characters, and realities await. Throughout this book we highlight and recommend important and fun anime and manga for you to try out, and while most of the shows and series are appropriate for all ages, please remember to always check in with a parent or guardian before you dive in! We'll be here with you every step of the way to assist you on your journey and to provide a road map to help you find your way.

Go beyond! Plus . . . ultraaaaa!

—SAMUEL SATTIN & PATRICK MACIAS

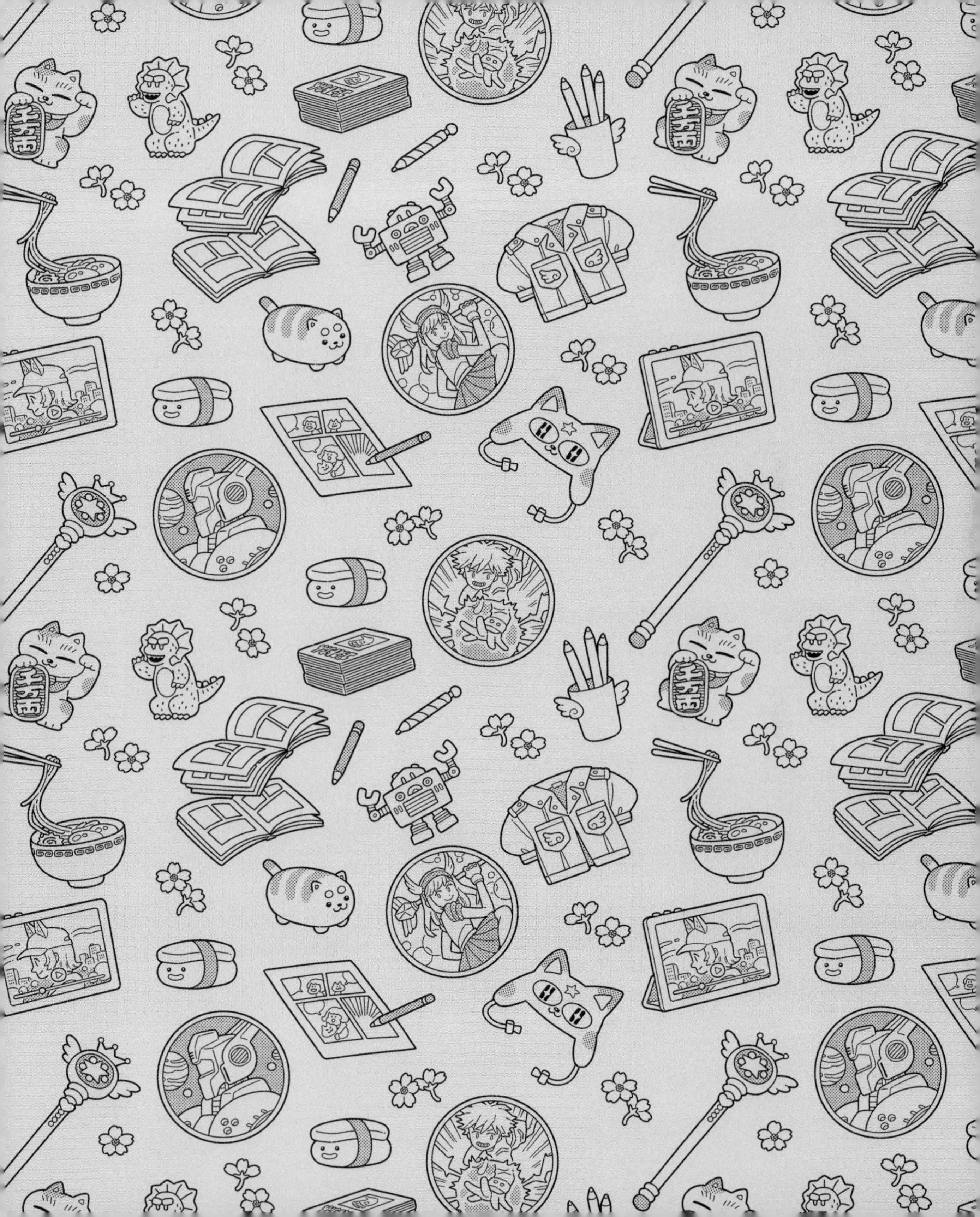

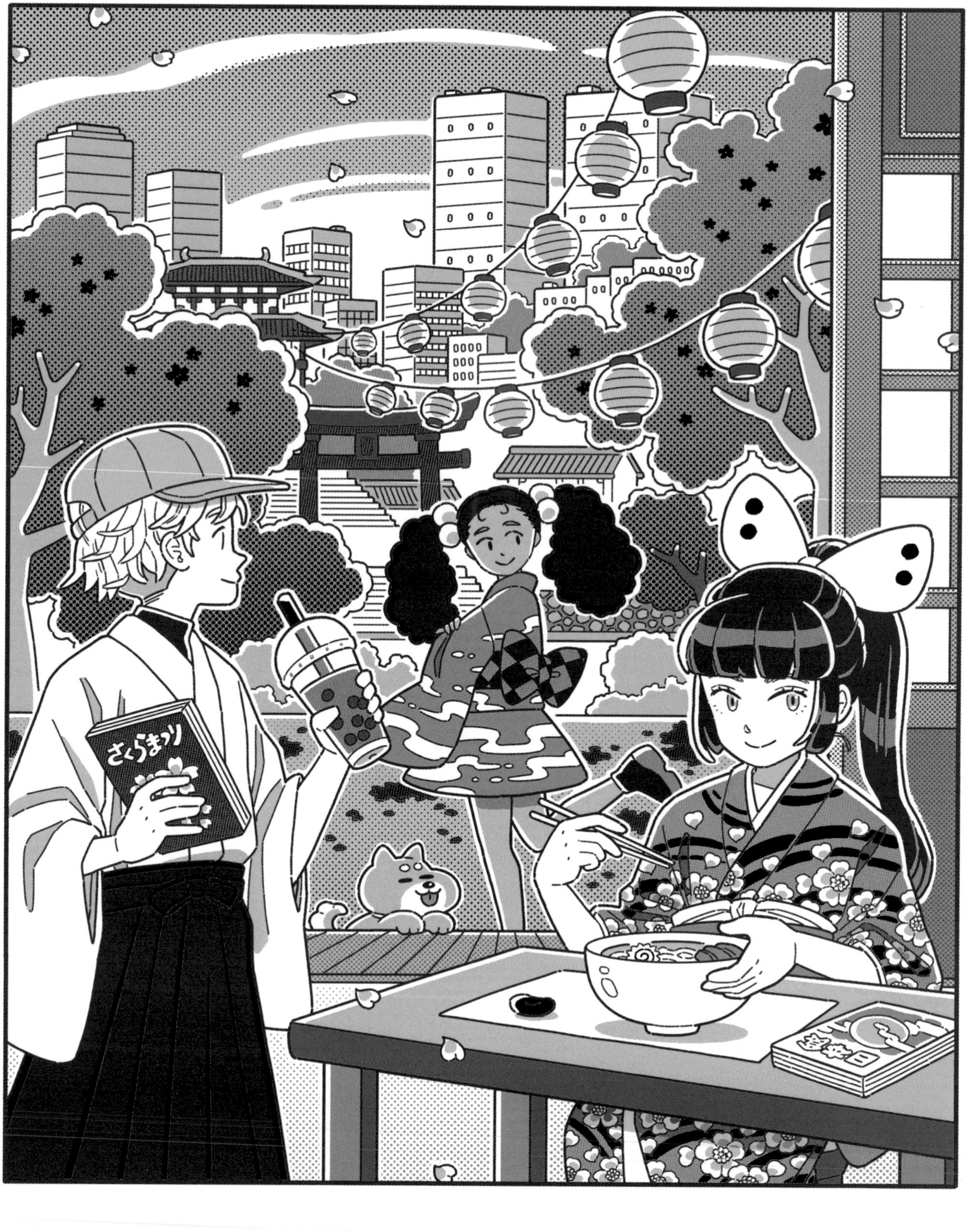
さくらまつり

CHAPTER 1

WELCOME TO JAPAN!

TODAY, ANIME AND MANGA CAN be watched and read all over the world. You might even be watching some anime right now or have a few manga series on your bedroom bookcase! It is great to be a fan of anime and manga, but it's important to remember that they came from Japan.

Why is that so important, though?

Well, since anime and manga started in and are made in Japan, it makes sense that many of the stories would take place in that country. So the more you know about Japan and Japanese culture, the more you can enjoy and appreciate your favorite characters and stories.

Let's begin with some basics!

THE LAND OF THE RISING SUN!

Japan is a country made up of four large islands—Hokkaido, Honshu, Shikoku, and Kyushu—and surrounding smaller islands. As far as actual size goes, Japan is not very big. Stretching 2,361 miles from north to south, it is about the same size as the state of California.

And with 125.5 million people living there (as of 2022), it can be crowded sometimes, especially in the big cities.

Some of the country's most famous cities include Sapporo, Osaka, Fukuoka, Okinawa, Kyoto, Nagoya, and Tokyo, which is also the national capital. And each of Japan's regions has its own unique customs, delicious foods, speech patterns, and ways of life.

Sitting between the Pacific Ocean and the Sea of Japan, the country falls along a series of underwater volcanoes in Asia known as the Ring of Fire. Earthquakes, both big and small, are very common in Japan because of all the volcanic activity.

Despite how scary it might sound to live surrounded by a bunch of volcanoes and amid frequent earthquakes, one of the country's most famous landmarks is Mount Fuji, an inactive volcanic mountain, which has become a symbol of the natural beauty of Japan. "Fujisan," meaning "Mt. Fuji," is a common nickname for this celebrated mountain. A time-honored tradition is to climb Mount Fuji overnight to view the sunrise from the mountain's peak, a journey that takes about five to seven hours. Some people prefer to take their time and do the climb over the course of two days. That means there's more time to enjoy the amazing scenery!

JAPANESE: THE LANGUAGE OF ANIME AND MANGA!

After all those hours spent reading manga, you might decide that you want to learn to read or write in Japanese. If so, that's great! Before you begin, it's important to know that there are three different writing systems in Japanese, and you'll need to be familiar with all of them.

There are two types of writing systems: one is based on syllables—like we are familiar with in English—and the other is made up of *ideograms*, which means that each character is built up from different shapes and has its own meaning while also corresponding to a word. The syllabic writing system is broken down further into an alphabet for Japanese words called *hiragana* and an alphabet for words borrowed from foreign languages, such as English, called **katakana.** Hiragana and katakana both have forty-six different characters, each with their own sound. Around first grade, kids in Japan learn how to read and write by first studying hiragana and katakana. They sound things out just like you learned to do. (So, once you learn katakana, you will be able to sound out words and recognize the ones that were borrowed from English. But there will also be other languages like French and German thrown in there too!)

Then there are the ideograms, called *kanji*. This system of writing came from China in the sixth century. There are about 2,000 different kanji you need to know to read Japanese easily—that's a lot to memorize! (And there really is no way around it . . .) Some kanji are easy to read and write, while others are more complex, requiring as many as twelve different strokes of a pencil or brush to complete.

Standard written Japanese includes a combination of all three forms: kanji, katakana, and hiragana. So you'll have a lot of practicing to do!

If you want to hear how the Japanese language sounds, and maybe pick up some phrases, watching untranslated anime will help a lot. One thing to keep in mind is that Japanese has different levels of speech based on who you are talking to. It's fine to speak casually with friends and close family, but you need to be extra polite and sometimes use entirely different words when dealing with people like teachers or an elderly neighbor. All this may sound like a lot to keep track of, but if you pay close attention to how characters talk to each other in different situations in anime, you might just get the hang of it. To be sure, manga and anime can be great study tools for learning Japanese!

IT'S A TRADITION!

With a culture that is thousands of years old, Japan has a number of unique traditions that often find their way into anime and manga.

CHERRY BLOSSOMS

Every spring in Japan, people gather outside to view the beautiful cherry blossoms (known as *sakura*) that bloom from the trees—but only for a very short period of time, which is why cherry blossoms have come to symbolize the fleeting joys of life. It's fun to gather with friends and family and have a *hanami*, or "flower viewing" party. Cherry trees in bloom, along with their falling petals, have been in too many anime and manga to mention, but some favorites include *Fruits Basket*, *Komi Can't Communicate*, and (naturally) *Cardcaptor Sakura*!

MATSURI

Local festivals in Japan are known as *matsuri*. Often held at temples and shrines in the simmering heat of summer, people celebrate these festivals by wearing light cloth robes known as *yukata* and enjoying special food from vendors like shaved ice, grilled corn, and pancake-like *okonomiyaki*. Special games (like catching goldfish) and ceremonial group dances are common, and sometimes the festivities are capped off with spectacular fireworks displays! You can find matsuri anime scenes in such titles as *Free!* and *The Melancholy of Haruhi Suzumiya*.

MARTIAL ARTS

Japan has developed a number of unique fighting and self-defense techniques that strengthen not only the body, but also the mind. Judo and karate are two of the best known Japanese martial arts that are practiced around the world. There's also kendo, which is a kind of sword fighting with bamboo poles. Kendo is sometimes taught in Japanese schools, along with kyudo, a kind of longbow archery. Both kendo and kyudo sometimes pop up in school-based anime. One Japanese martial art that is often seen in anime and manga is ninjutsu, the mysterious way of the ninja.

GAMES PEOPLE PLAY

From playing cards and board games to tests of strategy, there are a number of uniquely Japanese games that you'll find in anime and manga.

Shogi is a game that's similar to chess in that two players take turns in the hopes of capturing the other player's pieces. Although it's been around for thousands of years, there's been a recent shogi craze in Japan, helped in part by shogi-themed anime like *When Will Ayumu Make His Move?*

Loved by gamblers and outlaws, *hanafuda* is a card game featuring colorful artwork of animals and flowers. *Hana* means "flower" in Japanese. The game itself dates back to the eighteenth century. Tanjiro in *Demon Slayer* wears a pair of hanafuda cards as earrings.

Karuta is another Japanese card game, this time involving matching cards and proverbs. Since karuta often have short written sentences on the cards, they are sometimes used to teach young kids how to read. (Fun fact: Video game giant Nintendo actually began as a company that made karuta cards!) If you want to know more about karuta, the anime and manga series *Chihayafuru* is a great place to start!

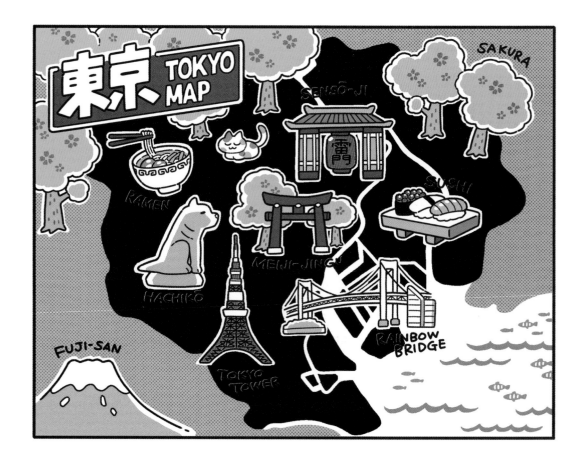

BRIGHT LIGHTS, BIG CITY!

Japan's capital city is Tokyo. With over thirteen million people living in its twenty-three wards, or districts, it's one of the largest and most populated cities in the world. Many anime studios, such as Toei and Ghibli, can be found in Tokyo. And there are lots of animators and manga artists who call Tokyo their home.

Here's just a sample of some of the highlights the city has to offer!

HARAJUKU

For decades, Harajuku has been Tokyo's colorful center of youth fashion. Every weekend, people come from all over Japan to meet friends, make new ones, and to check out the latest trends in the Harajuku neighborhood. There are big brand apparel shops here, but the real fun comes from exploring the hundreds of independently owned stores full of unique vintage clothing and wild new styles. It's a great people-watching spot on the weekend, and if you have a sweet tooth, you simply have to try one of the oversize sweet crepes for sale on Takeshita Street right across from Harajuku Station. Harajuku and the surrounding neighborhood sometimes pop up in anime such as *Paradise Kiss* and *Artiswitch*.

SHIBUYA

Packed with people, loud sounds, and bright lights, Shibuya is one of Tokyo's major shopping and entertainment hubs. Offering dance clubs, **karaoke** rooms, and plenty of fashionable stores and restaurants, it seems like the party never stops here. Still, if you prefer a little peace and quiet, take a short walk from Shibuya Station to the quiet greenery of Yoyogi Park.

One of Tokyo's most famous landmarks can be found in this district: Shibuya Crossing. This is an extremely busy traffic intersection in front of the train station where an estimated 2,500 people cross the street every time the lights turn green. Shibuya Crossing and the surrounding area often show up in anime and manga, including the 2015 film *The Boy and the Beast*.

AKIHABARA

Imagine a whole neighborhood filled with the latest anime goods like figures and collectibles, video games, and stacks of manga! Dream no longer, because such a place exists in Tokyo's Akihabara district. People from around the world visit Akihabara (or AKB as the locals sometimes call it) to shop and interact with other fans. In some ways, it feels like a giant year-round anime convention! As you might expect, stories set in Akihabara are very common in anime and manga. Some memorable ones include *Steins;Gate* and *Akiba's Trip: The Animation*.

NAKANO BROADWAY

While Akihabara specializes in the latest anime, manga, and gaming trends, fans in search of rare older items might do well to visit an indoor mall in Tokyo's Nakano neighborhood called Nakano Broadway. Here, you'll find hundreds of small specialty shops with figures and goods from anime and manga of the past. If there's a rare Pokémon card from the 1990s or a vintage Gundam kit from the 1980s you've spent a long time looking for, there's a good chance you might find it here!

THE GHIBLI MUSEUM

Located near a park in Mitaka, on the west side of Tokyo, this charming museum is dedicated to the work of award-winning anime director Hayao Miyazaki and the company he cofounded, Studio Ghibli. In addition to special exhibits and a replica animation studio, there are special Ghibli-themed foods and a gift store that will thrill fans of Miyazaki's works like *My Neighbor Totoro* and *Spirited Away*.

ANIME AND MANGA ARE EVERYWHERE!

Even if you're not in Tokyo, you don't have to go very far to find anime or manga in Japan. In fact, you'll find familiar characters from longtime classics like *Dragon Ball* and *Sailor Moon* to the latest hits like *My Hero Academia* and *Jujutsu Kaisen* just about everywhere you look!

From supermarkets to convenience stores and vending machines, anime characters are used to sell all kinds of products from snacks and drinks to household items. If you've ever wanted to eat *SPY x FAMILY* gummy candy or slurp on *Demon Slayer* instant noodles, then Japan is the place for you.

Meanwhile, on the trains or even while walking through a small town, it's common to see signs and posters of famous anime characters, such as *Gundam* and *Attack on Titan*, used in public service messages reminding citizens about safety and the importance of good manners.

Anime is truly everywhere in Japan!

—— TRANSLATOR SPOTLIGHT ——

INTERVIEW WITH JOCELYNE ALLEN

Jocelyne Allen is a Japanese translator and interpreter who splits her time between Toronto and Tokyo. She has translated hundreds of short stories, novels, and manga, including the Eisner Award–winning title *Lovesickness* by Junji Ito and the classic shojo manga *The Rose of Versailles* by Riyoko Ikeda.

What was the first manga you ever read?

> In English, it was probably *Sailor Moon*, back in the day when it was being published in *MixxZine*. In Japanese, I think it was *Chibi Maruko-chan*.

When did you start translating manga? Can you describe how you got into doing that?

> I started translating manga about fifteen years ago. I was already a translator, working on things like engineering papers and legal contracts, but I've always loved comics. So I wanted to branch out into manga if I could. I emailed some publishers. A couple took a chance on me, and I've been working on manga ever since.

In this book, we discuss how anime and manga are more available than they used to be, particularly to people in the United States. Why do you think that is?

> I think a large part of it is due to the rise of the internet and the accessibility of information about manga and anime. When I first got into this stuff, you kind of had to know someone who knew someone who had a bootleg VHS copy of some anime recorded off TV in Japan. But it's so much easier now to come into contact with anime and manga and discover your new true love.

What advice would you give kids who are looking to get into manga/anime? Where should they start?

> Look for stories you love. The great thing about manga and anime is that there is a story for everyone. So if you're into mysteries already, try picking up a mystery manga like *Case Closed*. Or if you've always been a huge cat lover, you can find all the cats you want in a series like *Chi's Sweet Home*. Once you start digging in, you'll find that one book almost inevitably leads to another, and before you know it, you'll be a manga expert.

What is your favorite manga and why?

> I could never pick just one manga. There are so many great books that speak to me in so many different ways. I love Shirai Yumiko's science-fiction saga *Wombs* for its incredible world-building and gorgeous art. Kyo Machiko's *Cocoon* breaks my heart every time I read it, with her empathetic and fantastical telling of the young girls caught up in the Battle of Okinawa. *Kaze to Ki no Uta*, Takemiya Keiko's magnum opus, astounds me with the sheer scale of emotion she manages to cram into every page. And Takahashi Rumiko's *Maison Ikkoku* is a book I go back to over and over again for its perfect balance of humor and reality and its depiction of learning to live with loss and finding love.

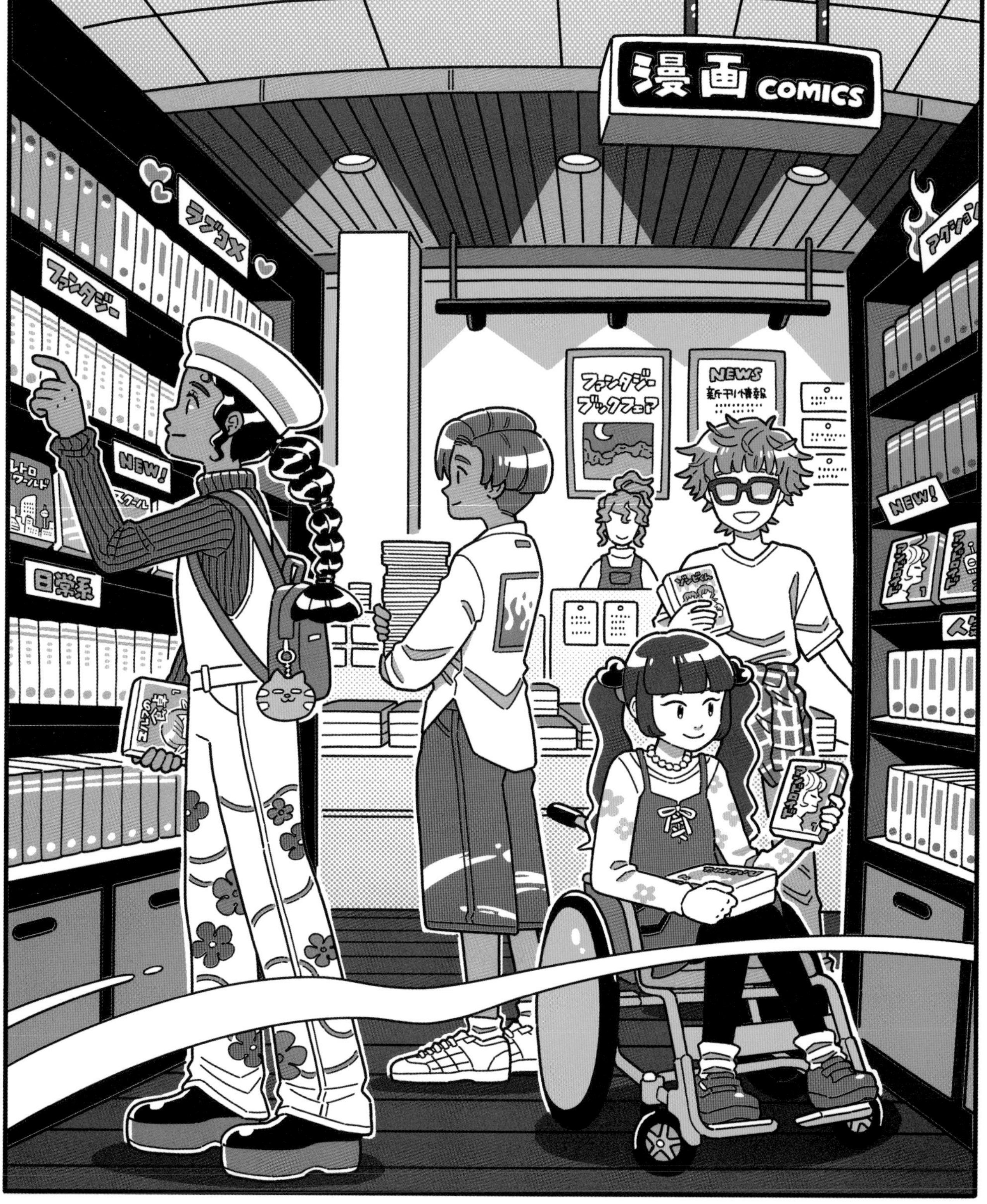
漫画 COMICS
ラブコメ
ファンタジー
アクション
NEW!
日常系
ファンタジー ブックフェア
NEWS 新刊情報
NEW!

CHAPTER 2

MOUNTAINS OF MANGA!

YOU'VE PASSED THEM IN STORE windows and in the stacks at local libraries. You've seen people poring over volumes of *Demon Slayer* and *Dragon Ball Super* in the aisles of your favorite local bookstore. You may overhear fellow classmates discussing *Yotsuba&!* before class, or you might spy your friends scrambling to get a hold of the latest volume of *Jujutsu Kaisen*. You might even be interested in joining a manga club or starting one yourself!

If any of this sounds familiar or exciting to you, then you have come to the right place.

You're going to hear a whole lot about anime in this book, which is awesome, but it's important to know that, without manga, there'd be a lot less anime out there. This is because, when it comes to Japanese pop culture, manga lies at the center of all things. In fact, while there are certainly some original anime shows being made, the majority of the anime you see has been directly adapted from manga and often follows the story lines beat by beat.

But before we get that far, let's answer the burning question: What *is* manga?

In Japanese, the word *manga* (used for both singular and plural) is made up of two Japanese characters, or kanji. The first is 漫, or *man*, which means "whimsical" or "impromptu." The second is 画, or *ga*, which means "pictures." So then, *manga* (漫画) as a whole ends up meaning something along the lines of "whimsical pictures." When you talk to Japanese speakers, however, they'll tell you that the closest English meaning is simply "comics." Why? Because that's what *manga* is—just another name for comics, but specifically the ones that come from Japan. These comics are drawn by **mangaka**, which is the Japanese word for a professional manga artist.

Okay, that can't be the only difference, right? If it is, then why would we have a whole chapter devoted to talking about just manga?

Well, manga definitely stands out from other comics created around the world because of the specific art style, storytelling, and production. Let's look at some of the ways that manga is similar to and different from traditional Western comics.

MANHWA AND MANHUA

It's worth noting that Korean comics (*manhwa*) and Chinese comics (*manhua*) have more similarities to Japanese comics than their Western counterparts. But manga continues to stand apart as unique stylistically in various ways.

WHAT MAKES MANGA . . . MANGA?

READING ORDER

One of the first things new readers of manga notice is that, unlike European and North American comics, manga is read from right to left—and back to front! On each page, you start at the top right-hand panel and read right to left, and top to bottom.

NAMING CONVENTIONS

When naming Japanese people, it is common in Japan to do so starting with the last name, followed by the first name. So, whereas in English we would be keen to write Osamu Tezuka when referring to the creator of *Astro Boy*, he would be referred to as Tezuka Osamu in Japan.

PANELS

While European comics tend to have only square panels, and American comic panels can take on all kinds of forms, Japanese comics usually rely on a more specific pattern of about five to six panels per page. The panels are often shaped in a variety of ways—from squares and rectangles to more interesting forms and even full- and double-page splashes—in order to pump up the action and drama.

BLACK AND WHITE

Manga's black-and-white look isn't just the industry standard; it also helps these comics stand apart stylistically. One of the reasons why manga is printed in black and white is that it's cheaper to do so. Color printing costs more, and sticking to black ink on a white page means it's easier to produce more pages. But that's not the only reason manga comes in black and white. When you don't have color to rely on, illustrations have to be more expressive and exact, which is one of the reasons why manga is so heavily detailed, with an immense amount of thought being paid to every part of a panel.

"Japanese people like to recognize and perceive things in outline forms—as lines. There are, in contrast, other peoples in the world who like to perceive things in terms of volumes or solid shapes. . . . There is, therefore, a physical reason that Japan mass produces and consumes manga as black-and-white line drawings."

—HAYAO MIYAZAKI, FROM "MY THEORIES ON THE POPULARITY OF MANGA" IN *TURNING POINT 1997–2000*

DETAIL

All comics the world over are elaborately drawn and exhibit a lot of detail in terms of line-work, but manga readers are often surprised by the amount of fully illustrated backgrounds there are in each story line, which can make the setting in these books feel bigger and more fleshed out.

ENDLESS GENRES

Manga stretches across more genres and subgenres than you can even imagine, and this art form is often the source of exciting new ones. (**Isekai**, anyone?) From sci-fi, fantasy, and horror to comedy, **slice of life**, romance, nonfiction, and drama, manga is never limited to just one kind of story. Western comics have been expanding into new genres in recent years as well, but they still are most often associated with superheroes, so they have a ways to go before they get to the manga level.

SO. MUCH. MANGA.

In Japan, the process of producing manga has been honed over the last sixty years. With a production process that pushes out loads of new books on a daily basis, there's a seemingly endless supply of stories awaiting readers. Some manga shops in Japan house multiple floors full of just manga, and it can feel a little overwhelming to figure out where to start or what series to explore first if you're new to reading them.

POCKET-SIZE

Did you know that the manga you get in the United States is printed on a physically bigger page than the original books manufactured in Japan? In Japan, manga are deliberately printed to fit in your pocket so that it's convenient to carry them around. There are exceptions, like magazine anthologies and digital manga, but most tankōbon—the word typically used to refer to manga volumes—are much smaller than you might expect.

EDITOR AT THE HELM

Editors play a much bigger role in manga than they do in other comics industries around the world. This is not to say that Western editors aren't involved with their books, but in Japan, manga editors are thought to contribute more than 30 percent of what goes into making a series really take off! They also connect with readers, conducting surveys to find out what people are interested in, so they can take that information back to their publishing companies to create marketable new stories or series.

IMPORTANCE OF MANGA

Manga is a well-respected art form in Japan. In the United States, comics are still gaining wider appreciation as a serious medium despite how popular they are. In Japan manga is a normal part of daily life and an important piece of the larger anime industry mentioned at the beginning of this chapter.

SERIALIZATION

Much like how issues of comics come out before the larger bound book editions, new manga comes out in chapters that are published in magazine anthologies, called *manga zasshi*. They are printed on newsprint, a type of paper that is very cheap to make, which makes it easier for more fans to purchase them regularly. In many of these magazines, especially popular ones like *Weekly Shonen Jump*, there are comment cards for readers to fill out. Unlike U.S. comic readers, manga fans can send their thoughts and opinions about the manga chapters and series they like the most to the editors. In many cases, the manga magazine and editors will often decide to keep or cut a series based on how much readers like it!

———— MANGA SPOTLIGHT ————

INTERVIEW WITH KAMOME SHIRAHAMA

Kamome Shirahama began as a manga artist with her series *Eniale & Dewiela* at Beam Comics. Also an illustrator, she has created multiple variant covers for Marvel and DC. Her internationally best-selling manga series *Witch Hat Atelier* is serialized on Kodansha's *Monthly Morning Two,* and she was the character designer for the story "The Elder" in the animation anthology *Star Wars: Visions.*

生まれてはじめて読んだマンガはなんですか？

What was the first manga you ever read?

> あまりよく覚えていませんが、手塚治虫のジャングル大帝だった気がします。
>
> I am not sure, but I think it was Osamu Tezuka's *Jungle Emperor* (ジャングル大帝).

いつマンガ家になりたいと思いましたか？　またその理由を教えていただけますか？

When did you decide you wanted to become a mangaka? And why?

> 高校生の頃にはもうマンガを描いていましたが、なり方もよくわからないし、現実的ではない夢だと諦めていました。大学時代に実際に漫画家として活躍している人と知り合って、自分でも目指せるのかも？と思ってから、考えるようになったと思います。

I was already making manga when I was in high school but did not know how to become a mangaka and thought it was an unrealistic dream. When I was in college, I met a mangaka who was established in the industry and thought that I might be able to become one. It was then that I started to truly think about it.

マンガ業界でのお仕事されるということはどんなものなのでしょうか?

What is it like working in the manga industry?

基本的には連載漫画を継続して描いて収益を得ていますが、イラストレーションとして本の挿画やゲームのスチル、キャラクターデザインの仕事を依頼される事もあります。連載原稿を入稿したら次の締め切りが来るまでの間にイラストの仕事をしています。

I basically have a manga series that I continue working on and make a living with, but I also am asked to work on one-shot illustrations for video games or character designs. After I am done with my monthly series, I work on other illustrations.

世界的に人気を博している「とんがり帽子のアトリエ」ですが、この作品のアイディアはどこから来たのでしょうか?

Where did you come up with the idea for your internationally acclaimed series *Witch Hat Atelier*?

今までに有名な魔法使いが主人公の作品は . . . 全てがそうとは言いませんが . . . 出自や血統で特別な力を使えるという設定のものが多くて、平凡な生まれのキャラクターはたとえ憧れても魔法使いにはなれないの?と、子供の頃疑問に思ったことがあります。そして大人になってから友人が「絵を描く工程って魔法みたいだよね」と言っているのを聞いて、魔法のような凄い技術を本当に魔法という設定にしてしまえば、誰でも魔法使いになれるんじゃない?というか、そのことに気づいてないだけで、実は誰もが魔法使いなんじゃない?と思いついたことがきっかけです。そこから世界を広げていきました。

Many older stories with witches as protagonists feature characters that have special powers due to their bloodline. So as a child, I wondered why an ordinary character couldn't become a witch if they wanted to. When I was a little older, a friend of mine told me that "the process of drawing a picture is like magic." Hearing that, I wondered why I couldn't use that concept to create a world where anyone can become a witch. That was the very start, and from there, I expanded the world.

現在アニメ化も進んでいる「とんがり帽子のアトリエ」ですが、そちらにも関わっているとのことですが、アニメとマンガのお仕事の大きな違いはなんでしょうか？

Now that you are also working on an anime adaptation of *Witch Hat Atelier,* what would you say the big difference is between working in anime and manga?

アニメに関しては . . . たくさんの人が関わって作るので、私からはまだ詳しいことをお伝えできません、すみません。でも、漫画よりも関わる人がより多くなっている部分が違いとしては一番大きいかもしれませんね。

For the anime, many people are involved, so I cannot say anything at the moment, I am sorry. But maybe the fact that there are so many people involved compared with manga is one big difference.

アニメやマンガのお仕事をしたいと思っている子供たちにアドバイスをするとしたらどのような言葉を送りますか？

What advice would you give kids who are looking to get into manga/anime?

学生の頃の私は、5年後の自分がどんな絵を描けるようになっていたいかを想像して、未来に習得しておきたい技のためにその時描く絵を決めていました。アニメやマンガの仕事をしたくて、今何か絵や漫画を描いたり、アニメについて調べたり、動画や本でメイキングを見て学んだりしている人は既に挑戦の一歩を踏み出してます。未来を想像しながら、努力を継続してください。

When I was still studying, I imagined what kind of art I would be able to draw five years from where I was at the time. In order to evolve to that point, I would consider the crafts/techniques that would be necessary to get there. For those who want to work on anime and manga, if you are already drawing illustrations or manga of your own, or if you are studying anime or reading books, you have already made the first step. Please keep working hard while imagining what your future might be like.

あなたの一番好きなマンガはなんですか？

What is your favorite manga?

萩尾望都先生のSF短編『ユニコーンの夢』です。

Moto Hagio's short sci-fi story *Unicorn's Dream* (ユニコーンの夢).

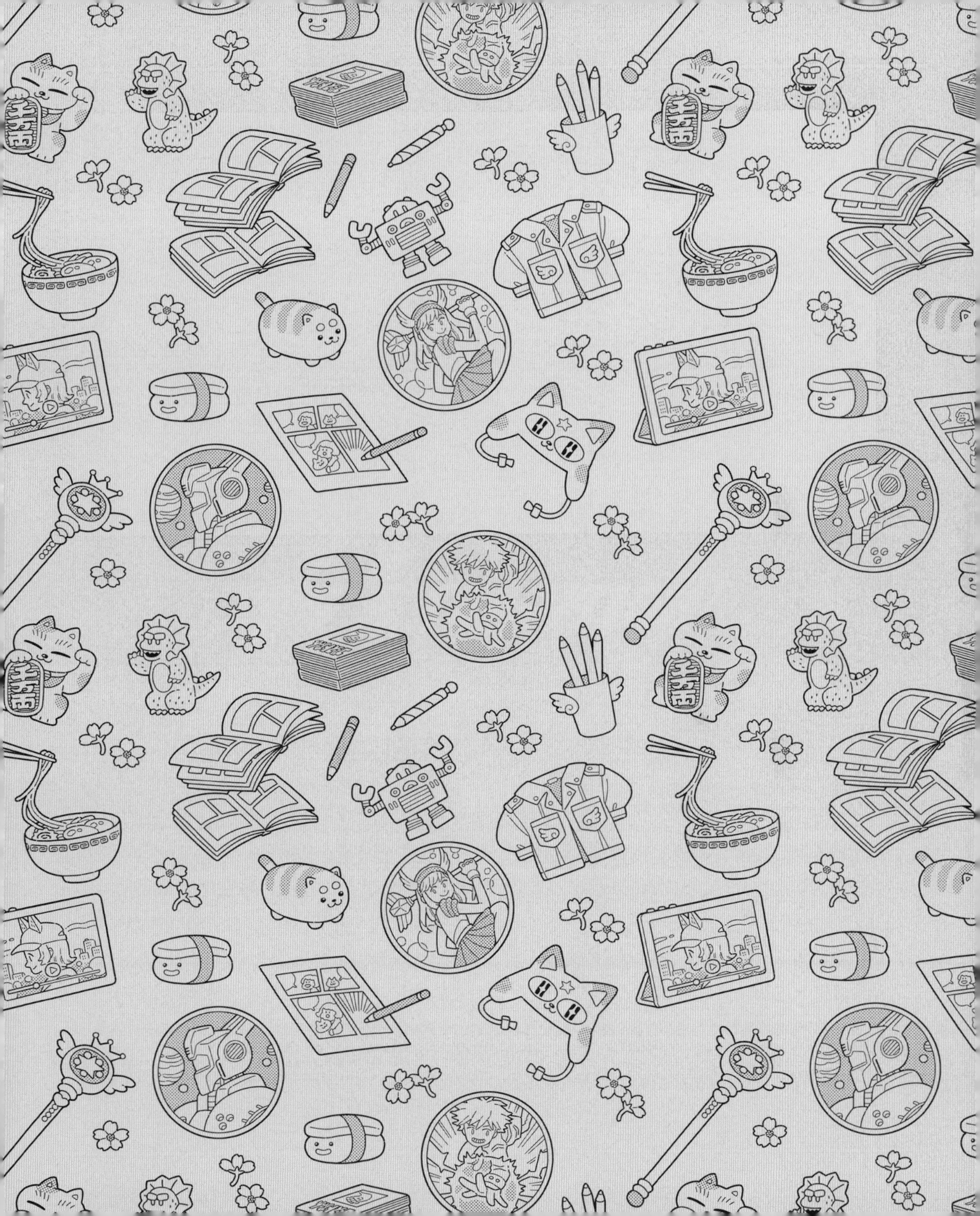

MAKING A MANGA

Creating manga is a complex and multilayered process. Let's have a look at the steps that go into some of your favorite comics:

1. An editor expresses interest in a story and sits down with the artist and/or writer to plot out the best path forward.

2. The artist draws what's called a **nemu**, or name, which is a rough sketch of the pages to come.

3. The real work begins with fleshing out the pages, characters, and story. Everyone is on deck, including the artist/writer and editor.

4. The pages are serialized in a magazine anthology. Readers vote to rank the popularity of each series.

5. Series that are unpopular are cut, while popular series continue. As more comics are produced, they are combined into tankōbon.

6. Anime adaptations of manga often begin after the series has at least a few stand-alone volumes out, so that the manga stays ahead of the show.

NEVER GIVE UP!
THE HISTORY OF MANGA

The Japanese created narrative scrolls during the country's Heian and Kamakura periods. This is why manga is thought to date back to twelfth-century Japan, with scroll drawings known as *toba-e* being read from left to right. Though modern manga began to develop in the nineteenth century and came together as we know it today in the early to mid-twentieth century with the likes of the "God of Manga" Osamu Tezuka, who we'll get to shortly, it's interesting to see how the blueprint for modern Japanese comics stretches back hundreds of years.

The most famous example of early manga is the Chōjū-jinbutsu-giga, or "Animal Scroll." Can you spot some of the similarities between this and modern manga?

For starters, you read this left to right. Also, the panels! This scroll tells a story, which is the primary role of manga. Additionally, this scroll contains **fukidashi**, or speech bubbles, and sequential storytelling.

In the late 1700s, during the artistically expressive Edo period, *kibyōshi*, or illustrated novels, began to appear in Japan, mostly among wealthy, art-savvy members of society. They contained satirical, often political, messages, paving the way for modern manga. In 1862, for instance, *Japan Punch* came onto the scene. Following Japan's opening of its borders for international trade, *Japan Punch* became one the country's first newspapers and contained political cartoons. In 1902, the newspaper *Jiji Manga (Topical Manga)*, modeled after the Sunday funnies comics in American newspapers, carried this tradition even further.

Akahon, or red books, became popular in the late 1940s during the occupation of Japan by Allied forces following WWII. Printed in Osaka, these books were created on the cheap due to a depressed economy in Japan at the time. Sold at roadside stalls, they became an economical way to convey long-form stories. Osamu Tezuka's *New Treasure Island* was among these akahon, becoming a bestseller nationwide.

Manga began to make its way to the United States in the 1980s, mostly via VIZ Media. It's been popular in Europe since the 1970s—particularly in France—and has a large presence there to this day. But recently, global attention to manga has expanded more than ever before, and it continues to be the best-selling category in comics in the United States and to drive a massive industry worldwide.

MANGA MVPS!

Manga has a long and fascinating history filled with creators and businesspeople who have brought this medium to where it is today. Beginning with Osamu Tezuka, we've profiled a batch of manga MVPs to get you started!

OSAMU TEZUKA.

Everything in modern manga begins with Osamu Tezuka. Known in Japan as the "God/Father of Manga," Tezuka-sensei produced more than 150,000 pages of manga in his lifetime. He's known primarily in the United States for *Astro Boy* (titled *Mighty Atom* in Japanese). The character of Astro Boy is so well known that he has an official birthday in Japan! But Tezuka-sensei's works span far and wide, with some of his most famous being *Black Jack*, *Unico*, *Dororo*, and many manga for adults. Tezuka-sensei also single-handedly jump-started the anime industry, but he's best known for his devotion to manga, which he saw as a way to communicate with people all over the world.

FUJIKO F. FUJIO.

No matter where you are in the world, you've probably seen Doraemon, the blue robot cat from the twenty-second century, somewhere. That's because Doraemon is considered to be a cultural icon in Japan. He was appointed "anime ambassador" in 2008 by Japan's Foreign Ministry and is the very definition worldwide of a kids' manga character. Created by Fujiko F. Fujio, the pen name of manga artist team Motoo Abiko and Hiroshi Fujimoto, *Doraemon* tells the story of ten-year-old Nobita Nobi, a boy who is struggling to do well in school. During a particularly bad week for him, the robot cat Doraemon created by Nobita's relatives in the future is sent back through time to help the boy have a better life. *Doraemon* has gone on to inspire countless manga artists and is a great introduction to manga for young readers.

AKIRA TORIYAMA.

It's hard to go anywhere in the world without encountering some part of *Dragon Ball*, like noticing Goku, Piccolo, Bulma, or Gohan on film posters, books, or video game covers. Akira Toriyama is the master behind *Dragon Ball*, a series that has changed the world forever. But that's not his only accomplishment. Considered to be one of the great mangaka of all time, Toriyama is also the creator of the popular kids' manga series *Dr. Slump* and has designed classic video games like *Chrono Trigger* and the *Dragon Quest* series. He's been honored widely in Japan and abroad, and he credits Osamu Tezuka-sensei as inspiring his signature drawing style.

RUMIKO TAKAHASHI.

Rumiko Takahashi is arguably one of the biggest reasons why manga and anime became popular outside of Japan—and in the United States in particular. She is known for the creation of series like *Inuyasha, Urusei Yatsura*, and perhaps most famously, *Ranma ½*, which established a subgenre of manga known as harem comedy, in which multiple girls have a crush on one guy. As a young woman in 1978, Takahashi entered a male-dominated industry at twenty-one years old. Becoming a smash success as a mangaka, her books have sold more than 200 million copies worldwide, and the *Ranma ½* anime, in particular, helped **VIZ Media** make more manga available in the United States.

TAKASHI YANASE.

An incredibly famous writer, illustrator, and poet, Takashi Yanase is best known for the creation of *Anpanman*. This manga series tells the story of Anpanman, who fights for justice and saves as many people as he can from threats like his greatest enemies, Baikinman and Dokinchan. The comic ran for forty years and is considered one of the first classic kids' manga, eventually being developed into anime and heavily merchandised in Japan to this day.

YUDETAMAGO.

Yudetamago is the pen name of writer Takashi Shimada and artist Yoshinori Nakai. The duo is known for their famous creation *Kinnikuman* (meaning "Muscle Man" in Japanese), an over-the-top wrestling comedy/action/drama about a superhero wrestler named Suguru Kinniku who tries to keep the title of prince on the planet Kinniku. As a cornerstone of kids' manga, *Kinnikuman* can be found everywhere in Japan, and at one point it even made its way to North America in the form of toys.

CLAMP.

An all-female team, CLAMP is the collective studio name for writer Nanase Ohkawa and artists Mokona, Tsubaki Nekoi, and Satsuki Igarashi. The group met in the 1980s in high school and went on to create some of the biggest manga series of the 1990s and early 2000s. They're perhaps most famous for the adorable, forward-thinking *Cardcaptor Sakura*, and the slightly maturer *Chobits* and *xxxHolic*. An important part of manga history, CLAMP's work is worth reading, not only because of how many popular stories and characters they've created, but also because of the fact that they made history becoming the first all-women team in the industry.

IN CONCLUSION . . .

Today, the world of manga is huge, exciting, and more accessible than ever before. Remember: reading manga from an earlier decade won't just show you how far this medium has come. Reading early manga series will help you find stories that you'll be happy you didn't pass by and characters that will stay with you forever. And it will help you better understand where more recent manga truly came from.

THE ULTIMATE TOP 20 MANGA LIST

Here is an amazing list of what we feel are twenty of the all-time greatest manga! It's true that everyone has different opinions on what they consider great, but we promise that there's something here for everyone. So have a look and get reading! (Note: We did not include manga for mature readers, and all of the manga on this list is good for anyone under the age of thirteen.)

1. **DETECTIVE CONAN** by Gosho Aoyama: A long-running series that follows a high school prodigy detective/elementary school student (yes, we know that sounds confusing—but trust us, it works!) who solves mysteries with his school's Junior Detective Club.

2. **FRUITS BASKET** by Natsuki Takaya: An emotional, heartwarming story about a girl named Honda Tohru who discovers that her classmate and her classmate's family turn into zodiac animals when they're embarrassed, stressed, or hugged by someone of the opposite gender.

3. **MY HERO ACADEMIA** by Kohei Horikoshi: An action-packed, emotional story about a normal boy in a superpowered world, who inherits an incredible power from the greatest superhero, along with all the difficulties that come with it.

by Akira Toriyama: The world-famous series about a boy named Son Goku who is trying to search the world for mythical orbs called dragon balls.

by Tetsu Kariya and Akira Hanasaki: A brilliant, mouthwatering series about the thing that all humans can agree is delicious: food! Each book features different recipes while exploring what makes things delicious.

by Hayao Miyazaki: A sweeping masterwork by the creator of Studio Ghibli, this book tells a tale of a fragile world filled with toxic jungles and gigantic insects—and the girl who must save it from collapse.

by CLAMP: This renowned magical girl series follows ten-year-old Sakura on her journey to capture escaped magical Clow Cards, while showing off new fashion—as long as it's approved by her flying friend Cerberus.

by Kiyohiko Azuma: This lovely series explores the life of young Yotsuba as she and her family move into a new home, meet neighbors, and uncover local mysteries.

by Bisco Hatori: In this hilarious high school story, a lower-income girl at a school for the wealthy is forced to repay an $80,000 debt by working for the school's most elite, all-male club—while disguised as a boy! (Parental Guidance Suggested) by Yoshitoki Oima: A heartfelt, important story about bullying, disability, and how people can grow and change.

by Konami Kanata: Follow the adventures of the mischievous kitten named Chi as she learns about the world around her. Cat lovers, this is the series for you!

by Kata Konayama: This story is about a young, nonbinary kid who wants to find others like them to connect with and ends up working at a café run by queer staff.

by Naoko Takeuchi: This series is known worldwide for its famous Sailor Scouts who fight evil in the name of justice and Princess Serenity. You can't go wrong with *Sailor Moon*.

by Hiromu Arakawa: This epic and captivating tale takes place in a world where alchemy is a real and respected science and humans can change parts of themselves at great cost. Follow the adventures of Edward and Alphonse as they search for the Philosopher's Stone. (Parental Guidance Suggested)

by Eiichiro Oda: One of the longest-running and most popular manga series in the world, *One Piece* follows the adventures of a boy named Luffy who accidentally eats a Devil Fruit that gives his body the consistency of rubber. Adventures ensue.

by Kamome Shirahama: A lush
and magical tale of a girl who thinks she can't be a witch due
to a lack of powers . . . until she meets one who conjures
magic through drawing magical runes with enchanted ink.

by Mamoru Hosoda and
Renji Asai: Based on the popular film, this limited series
manga tells the story of a boy who, after the death of
his mother, wanders into a kingdom of beasts where he
is swept up in an epic tale of bravery and sacrifice.

by Yoh Yoshinari: At a prestigious
school for young girls training to be witches, young Atsuko
Kagari struggles to fit in due to her nonmagical background,
until she discovers a magic artifact that changes her entire life.

by Akira Toriyama: Set in Penguin
Village, *Dr. Slump* follows an inventor who builds what
he thinks will be the world's most perfect girl robot:
Arale Norimaki. She turns out to be anything but.

by Osamu Tezuka: The classic tale of a
boy robot who, after being abandoned by his maker, is
taken in by a kind scientist and then goes on to fight
in the name of truth, justice, and human rights.

—— MANGA SPOTLIGHT ——

INTERVIEW WITH DEB AOKI

Deb Aoki is a manga aficionada, storyboard artist, editor, and traveler. She covers manga for a variety of publications and cohosts the internationally renowned podcast *Mangasplaining*.

What was the first manga you ever read?

Hard to remember exactly, but the one I remember strongly is *Candy Candy* by Kyoko Mizuki and Yumiko Igarashi. It's a story about a cheerful girl who grows up in an orphanage and ends up being adopted by a wealthy family with very awful children and befriending other wealthy kids who are much nicer to her, with some ending up falling in love with her. It's a story that's full of exciting melodrama and romance, which, frankly, I wasn't getting from American comics for girls.

It had an animated series that aired in Japanese with English subtitles on a local TV station in Hawaii, so that added to my fascination with it. I ended up subscribing to the Japanese manga magazine where it was serialized, *Nakayoshi*, via one of the Japanese bookstores in Hawaii. Mind you, it was all in Japanese, and my Japanese reading skills were (and still are) pretty basic, but I could follow the story thanks to the very clear visual storytelling and some help from a Japanese-English dictionary.

When did you decide you wanted to write about manga?

Well, it actually happened kind of by accident.

I have some basic journalism experience, thanks to working in both my high school and college newspapers, and then eventually writing for the daily morning paper in Honolulu. So before I had thought of writing about manga, I was already pretty comfortable with being a journalist.

I got a job in the online publishing world, and then a colleague of mine encouraged me to check out the list of available subjects that the website About.com was seeking writers for. One topic listed happened to be manga, so I applied, wrote some sample articles, and got the gig.

Eventually, I was able to get a professional website up, print business cards, and introduce myself to different manga publishers, both by email and in person at anime/comic conventions. Since then, it's been a really fun and exciting journey—one that I would have never imagined would introduce me to so many interesting people, places, and experiences.

What is it like working as a reporter in the manga industry?

Well, it's kind of odd, you know? You'd think there would be a lot of people writing about manga since it's so popular. But it seems like there's a lot more focus on anime and Western comics in the pop culture journalism space in North America.

I'm familiar enough with anime and other types of Western comics. But I like focusing on manga—and lately, webtoons—because it makes it easier for me to follow trends and get the interview opportunities I'm most interested in pursuing. I've gotten to know a lot of the manga publishers in North America and have also gotten to know other reporters, writers, and podcasters who cover anime, comics, and manga. I regularly travel to Japan, and lately I have been exploring the manga scene in France through my trips to the Angoulême Festival there. I go wherever my curiosity takes me.

The other thing I should mention is that comics journalism in general pays pretty poorly. While it's possible to have comics journalism as a full-time job, in my case, it's something I do on the side. My day job is flexible enough, though, to allow me to pursue my passion for manga and comics in general.

Where did you come up with the idea for your hit podcast *Mangasplaining*? And what impact has it had on readers?

The idea for *Mangasplaining* came from a friend of mine, Christopher Butcher. We, along with some other manga friends, went on a trip to Japan in 2019. We went to the nerd shopping heaven Mandarake and to the Shotaro Ishinomori museums in Sendai. There is simply so much manga out there and so many stories and art styles to explore!

But when the COVID-19 pandemic hit, my friends and I suddenly weren't traveling as much as we used to. That's when Christopher suggested starting a podcast with the hook that we'd be introducing our friend Chip, who is pretty well-known both as a comics artist and writer, to manga, one book at a time.

And the timing was perfect because during the pandemic, manga sales just exploded! Anime played a big part of this too, as more people were watching anime on Netflix, Hulu, and Amazon Prime, not just anime fan-centric sites like Crunchyroll or HIDIVE. Another trend is that people were rediscovering manga that they've always been meaning to read.

So I guess *Mangasplaining* came along and gave people who were curious about manga an easy introduction to what's worth reading and a variety of stories. And because Chip, Christopher, and David are well respected by comics readers, creators, publishers, librarians, retailers, and bookstore professionals, they are able to offer insights that are fun and accessible for readers who aren't that into manga to begin with.

It's super-exciting that we're now expanding the scope of what we're doing to include manga publishing! We've announced two manga series so far that we'll either be serializing online and/or publishing as print editions with Udon Entertainment and Fantagraphics.

What advice would you give kids who are looking to get into manga/anime?

I guess the best place to start is to ask your friends what they're watching or reading, or ask your school or public librarian for suggestions. You can also check out online sites like Anime News Network or Crunchyroll News too.

The way I got into manga initially was through a book called *Manga! Manga!* by Frederik Schodt. It was first published in the early 1980s, and while it doesn't include information about today's current favorites, it does provide a lot of great information about manga's history and its cultural influence in Japan. I'm also a huge fan of the British Museum's book on manga. This one fills in a lot of the information with great interviews and examples of modern manga worth reading. Paul Gravett's books on manga are terrific too.

What are some of your favorite kids' manga and why? What did you grow up reading?

The manga I enjoyed as a kid . . . well, most of it isn't available in English for various reasons. But there are lots of kid-friendly manga that are worth reading. A classic is *Doraemon* by Fujiko F. Fujio—that's available in English as a Kindle-only digital release. This story about a nerdy boy who's not a great student but gets mentored by a robot cat from the future is so much fun to read.

I also recommend *Chi's Sweet Home,* a charming story about a kitten who gets adopted by a family, even though their apartment doesn't allow pets. *Witch Hat Atelier* is also another stellar pick. It's a beautifully drawn fantasy story about a young girl who's studying to be a witch under the care of a kind mentor, but also dealing with a secret society of not-so-nice witches who want to change how the world handles magic. *Yotsuba&!* is another fun one—a green-haired little girl and her adoptive father move to a new town and have fun, slice-of-life adventures that will make you laugh.

I also love, love, love sports manga. One favorite that I think younger readers will enjoy is *Medalist,* a story about a tween girl who has an ambitious goal: to be a world-class figure skater. My other favorite is *Haikyu!!,* which is about volleyball. This one is a long series, but is so, so rewarding in how the characters grow and change over time and the friendship that they share with both their teammates and rival teams.

What is your favorite manga and why?

I'm currently into *One Piece,* the long-running series about a rubber-limbed pirate and his globe-trotting adventures in a fantasy world. It takes a little time to get into, but once it gets going, you're in for a ride that you won't forget. There are moments when it will make you laugh out loud and moments when it'll bring tears to your eyes. It's everything you want manga to be—and once you get into it, you'll say, "Oh, so *that's* why it's the most popular manga in Japan."

Another manga that I'll read again and again is *Emma* by Kaoru Mori. Set in Victorian England, a maid falls in love with a young man from a wealthy, aristocratic family. While their feelings are mutual, the couple must overcome several barriers of class, tradition, and social circumstances to get to their hopefully happy ending. The art is stunning, and the story is really satisfying in almost every way.

Blue Giant is another current favorite. This series about a young man who discovers a passion for jazz while he's in high school is just a fun and fascinating read. The story takes him from his hometown in Sendai to Tokyo, and later, as the series continues, follows him to Europe and eventually to the place where jazz began in the United States.

Blank Canvas by Akiko Higashimura is also fantastic. This story follows Higashimura as she recalls her days as a high school student trying to get into art school and the no-nonsense art teacher who teaches her what making art is really all about. It's a short series, but it's both fun and heart-wrenching—even if you've never imagined going to art school, the storytelling is masterful and just a perfect mix of humor and heart.

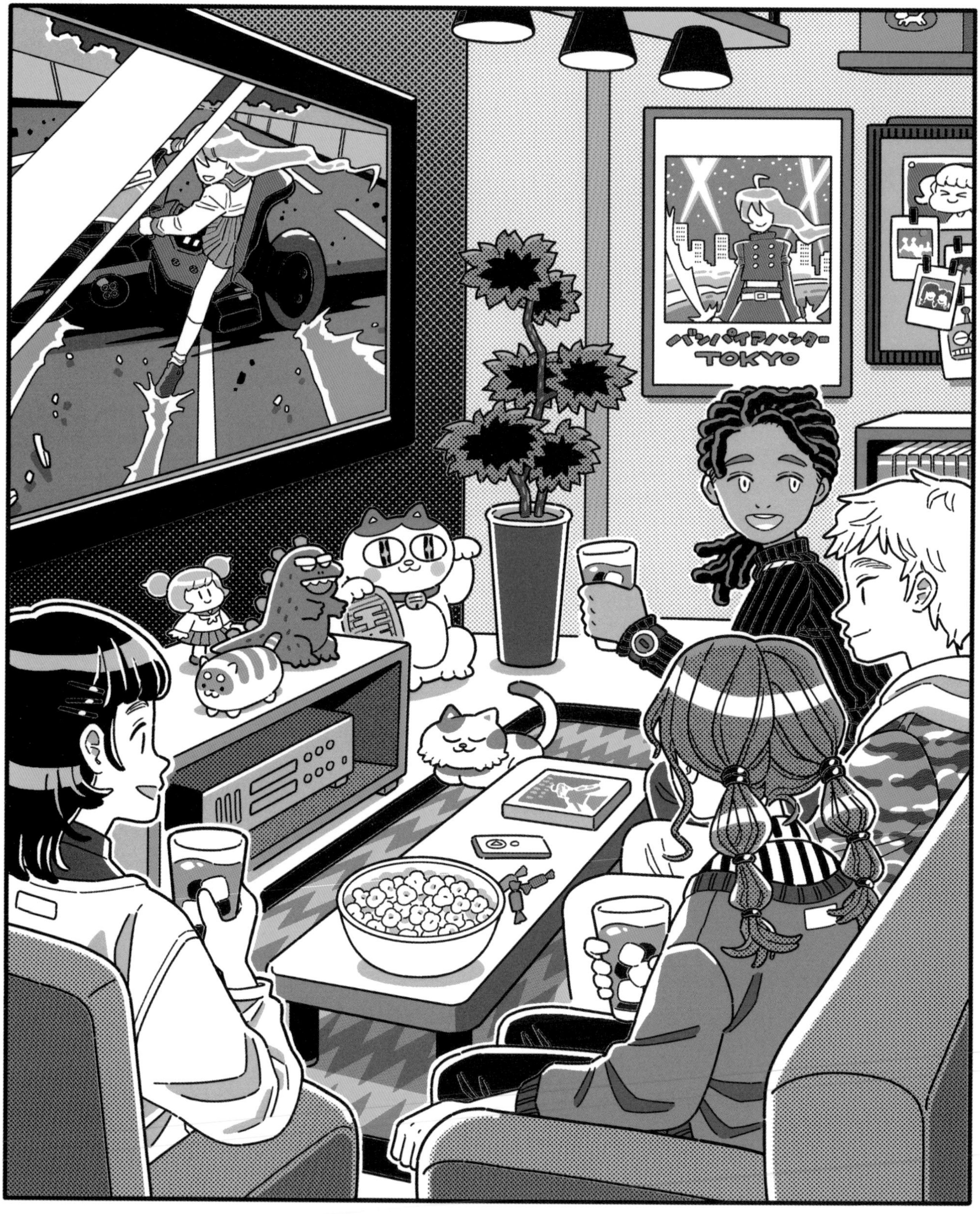
バンパイアハンター
TOKYO

CHAPTER 3

WHAT IS ANIME?

ANIME IS THE TERM FOR animation from Japan, and it's much more than just a form of entertainment to watch at home or at a movie theater. Anime is a cultural force, a very big business, and for millions of fans around the world . . . a way of life! No matter where you were or when you first discovered anime, it's important to remember that this is an art form with a long and fascinating history. It's fun to think about how anime evolved over the years . . . and where it might go next!

HOW IS ANIME MADE?

Japanese animation is made using individual drawings (known as **cels**), carefully sequenced together and photographed on film or digitally, to create the illusion of movement.

THE ORIGINS OF ANIME

According to some historical accounts, Japanese artists first began experimenting with animation around 1917. That's right! Anime is over one hundred years old!

Early animation in Japan used to be created by one person or a small team who made short films inspired by folktales or humorous jokes. Putting together animation was expensive and difficult during those early years, but creators had lots of fun experimenting with the possibilities of this new form of film entertainment.

During the years following World War II in the 1940s, there was a sudden flood of imported animated films in Japan from sources like Walt Disney (*Mickey Mouse* and *Snow White*) and the Fleischer Brothers (*Popeye* and *Superman*). These foreign cartoons had a massive impact on the people who saw them, including budding artist Osamu Tezuka. He, along with other artists of his generation, would soon plant the seeds of the anime revolution to come!

Meanwhile, new entertainment companies sprang up in Japan during the 1950s, including Toei, a film studio whose animation department would, decades later, help bring smash hit anime like *Dragon Ball*, *Sailor Moon*, and *One Piece* to the world.

ANIME ARRIVES ON TV

In 1960, Osamu Tezuka and Toei collaborated on a movie based on Tezuka-sensei's manga retelling of the classic legend *Journey to the West*. The next year, Tezuka would establish his very own animation studio, called Mushi Production. The ever-inventive Tezuka was interested in making high-quality and artistic animation, but he knew he also needed a hit, so Mushi Production developed the first TV anime series in Japan with an ongoing character: *Mighty Atom*—or *Astro Boy* as it came to be known around the world. These timeless adventures of a robot boy with human emotions first debuted on Japanese TV on January 1, 1963.

Television was still relatively new in Japan at the time, and shows were still only in black and white. But *Mighty Atom* was one of Japanese TV's first big hits, generating an avalanche of toys, records, and related merchandise for fans to buy and collect. The era of anime goods was born!

The success of *Mighty Atom* helped ignite a craze for children's animation in Japan. Tezuka and his staff created more new TV anime series based on his manga, including the first full-color animated TV series from Japan: *Kimba the White Lion* (fun fact: this series is said to have been an influence for Disney's *The Lion King*) and *Princess Knight*—one of the first **shojo** anime (anime specifically for girls).

Meanwhile, more manga creators made the jump to animated TV shows, including the Yoshida brothers who formed their own studio called Tatsunoko Production. They produced a worldwide hit of their own with *Speed Racer* in 1967.

At this point, the word *anime* was not yet being used to describe these early series, which were more commonly called "TV manga" in Japan. But one series would soon change all of that, breathing life into the anime that we now know and love.

WE'RE OFF TO OUTER SPACE!

Space Battleship Yamato first aired on Japanese TV in 1974. This was a serious science fiction animated series aimed at slightly older audiences than the previous TV manga shows. *Yamato* was set in the year 2199, and Earth was under attack from alien invaders. Our heroes had to make a long journey to another world to receive special technology that could save the planet. Unlike *Mighty Atom* or *Speed Racer*, every episode of *Space Battleship*

Yamato was meant to be watched in order. It was a long saga, with a beginning, middle, and end, but viewers—kids and adults alike—just couldn't get enough of it.

Seeing how popular this new kind of epic was, the studios realized there needed to be a new way to set it apart from TV manga. According to the documentary film *Space Battleship Yamato: The Making of an Anime Legend*, this is when the Japanese animation industry began calling these types of storytelling series anime.

MECHA MANIA!

Giant robots had been popular in Japan since the early animated TV series like *Mighty Atom* and *Gigantor* in the 1960s, followed by the action-packed "Super Robots" shows of the early 1970s like *Mazinger Z* and *Getter Robo*. These shows were mostly for younger audiences.

Mobile Suit Gundam, which debuted on Japanese TV in 1979, raised the stakes—and the average viewing age—for robot anime series. Similar to *Yamato*, with sci-fi concepts and life-and-death drama, it also had a more detailed setting and more complex characters, like the charismatic antihero Char Aznable and the reluctant teenage soldier Amuro Ray. The humanoid robotic **mecha**—known as "Mobile Suits"—that these characters piloted were made into real model kits that sold by the millions in Japan. These toys eventually helped *Gundam* become a giant symbol of anime around the world.

THE ANIME BOOM

Anime became a major cultural force in Japan during the 1980s. Anime movies were selling out theaters; anime theme songs became hit records; and anime **voice actors** became celebrities. Meanwhile, some anime fans were becoming more than just viewers. Creative

types began to develop their own amateur anime films. Others began to gather in the streets dressed as their favorite anime character—what is known as **cosplay**. Eventually, talented fans began entering the anime industry as professional creators.

For example, a show like *Super Dimension Fortress Macross* (1982) was put together in part by devoted fans who had grown up watching *Mighty Atom* and *Yamato*. The creators put jokes about and references to their favorite series and movies into their work, creating a kind of early "geek media" in the process.

Other anime creators wanted to use animation for new works that were both entertaining and highly artistic. Director Hayao Miyazaki, who had started as an animator at Toei, made a splash with his second film, *Nausicaä of the Valley of the Wind* (1984), which had a strong female hero and thoughtful environmental themes. Following this film's success, Miyazaki cofounded Studio Ghibli and went on to direct some of the most beloved anime hits of all time, including *My Neighbor Totoro* (1988) and *Kiki's Delivery Service* (1989).

ANIME GOES GLOBAL

With anime now exploding on Japanese TV, in the home video market, and in theaters, it was only a matter of time before it spread around the world. Anime's worldwide growth can partially be traced back to one particular movie. Based on the best-selling manga by Katsuhiro Otomo, *Akira* (1988) was the most technically dazzling anime of its time, presenting viewers with an eye-popping look at life in the dark, futuristic city Neo-Tokyo, complete with motorcycle gangs and psychic forces. *Akira* quickly became a must-see movie for science fiction fans around the globe, and people everywhere began to realize that some amazing things were happening in Japanese animation.

Curious viewers dug a bit further and discovered mind-expanding science fiction films like Mamoru Oshii's *Ghost in the Shell*. But there were *all kinds of anime* to enjoy, ranging from the thrilling superheroics of *Dragon Ball* and the dramatic sports saga of *Slam Dunk* to hit anime from female creators like Rumiko Takahashi (*Ranma ½*), Naoko Takeuchi (*Sailor Moon*), and the four-woman art group known as CLAMP (*Cardcaptor Sakura*).

There were still lots of anime for kids of course, like the smash hit *Pokémon* (1997), but there were also maturer works like the sci-fi cool of *Cowboy Bebop* and the experimental shojo anime *Revolutionary Girl Utena* (1997). Maybe the defining anime of the 1990s was *Neon Genesis Evangelion*. Coming from a studio created by anime fans, *Evangelion* took inspiration from the mecha shows of the past like *Gundam* and went to new places by exploring the inner lives and emotions of its main characters.

By the end of the 1990s, anime had risen to the next level both in Japan and around the globe. Everywhere, from North America to Europe, the Middle East, and everywhere in between, people loved anime! Fans held **conventions** to celebrate their favorite creators and characters together. Some fans even started their own anime and manga companies to help translate and distribute classic and new works.

In 2003, Hayao Miyazaki's *Spirited Away*, which is the story of a young girl forced to work for demons and spirits in a magical bathhouse, won the Academy Award for Best Animated Feature. This was a big moment, showing that anime could stand beside, and sometimes even outshine, works by the likes of other animation giants such as Disney.

Back in Japan, a whole new generation of anime heroes had sprung from the pages of **shonen** manga magazines, like *Naruto*, *Bleach*, *One Piece*, and *Fullmetal Alchemist*. These shows combined action, comedy, drama, and memorable characters to great effect and won fans all over the world.

ANIME EVERYWHERE, ALL THE TIME!

There was just one problem with anime's global appeal . . .

Fans could not get the latest episodes of their favorite shows fast enough! In the days of TV and home video, there was usually a time lag between when fans in Japan could view new episodes of their favorite anime and when viewers overseas could see them with **subtitles** or **dubbed** into different languages.

But the internet changed everything. Companies like Crunchyroll began simulcasting the latest anime shows from Japan, making subtitled episodes available to viewers hours after broadcast.

Once anime became even more available, it became more popular than ever! Thanks to social media, fans could also share their interests in huge numbers and interact with Japanese creators and anime studios in real time. Celebrities like musicians Pharrell Williams and Ariana Grande began to go public with their love of anime and Japanese pop culture. And why shouldn't they? There's a lot to be excited about!

Yet Japanese animation now faces many challenges, too. Despite the popularity of anime around the world, pay for many workers in the industry remains low and deadlines are stressful. Some animators want to see the industry offer a better work-life balance. There's a lot of room for improvement!

Still, every few months, dozens of new anime are released for fans to enjoy. Some go on to become big hits that change the trajectory of the industry. Recent highlights include the smash hit movie *Your Name.*, as well as the TV anime series *Demon Slayer* (one of the most popular anime in recent memory) and *SPY x FAMILY*. Meanwhile, classic franchises like *Mobile Suit Gundam* and *Macross* are always getting new sequels for viewers who are fans for life. Anime is here to stay!

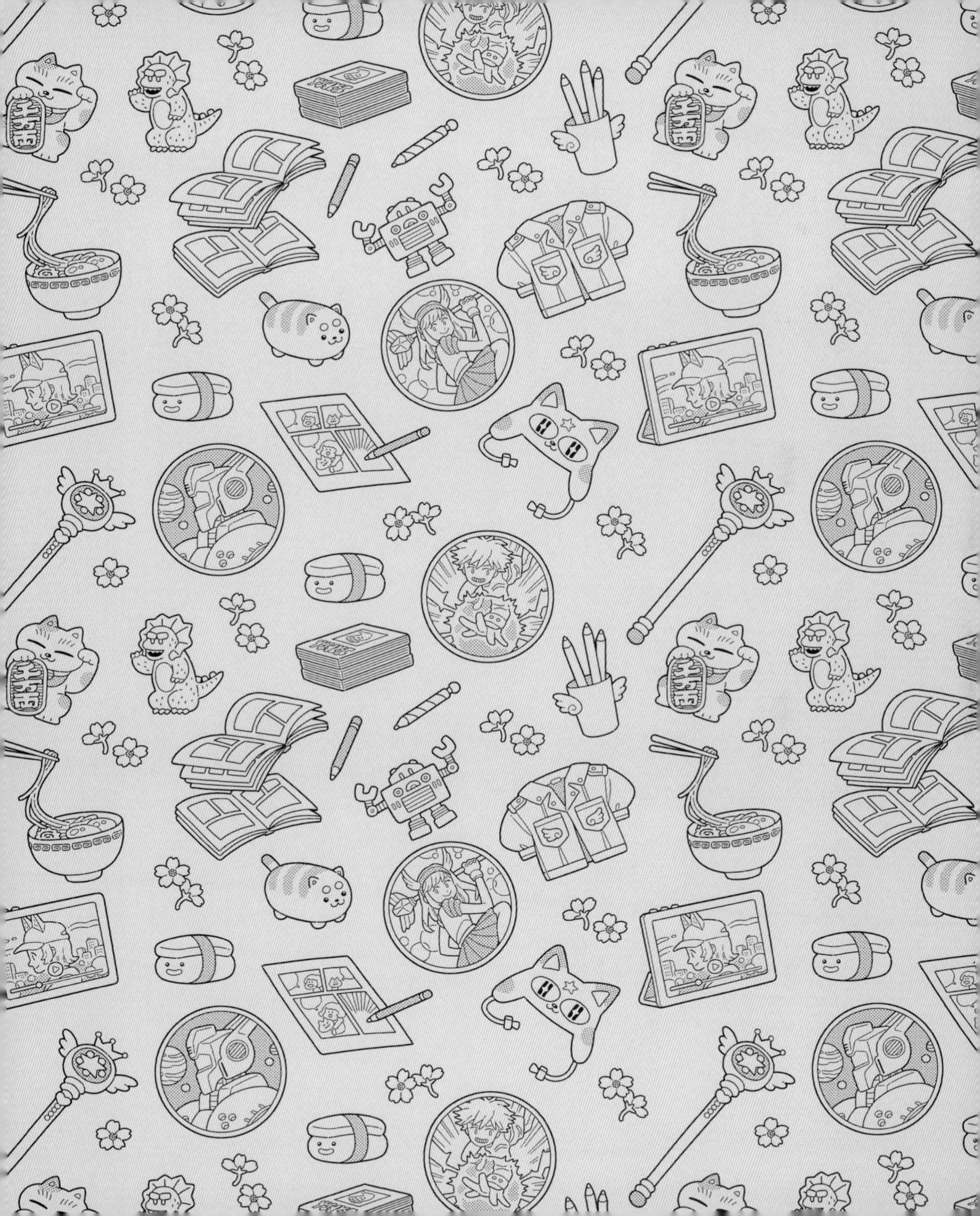

WHAT KIND OF
MANGA/ANIME IS FOR YOU?

If you're having a little trouble deciding where to begin with manga and anime, take this quiz! Circle whichever answers feel best for you right now, and don't worry if you're having trouble making choices. You can also pick more than one answer for each question if you want. And remember: there's no right answer—just fun to be had!

In your free time, you're most likely to do which of these things?

    A. Go outside and play an athletic game with your friends

    B. Go to the library to explore new books

    C. Sit down to play a game of chess

    D. Play video games

    E. Open your sketchbook and start drawing

    F. Go to a bookstore and/or comics shop

The kind of stories you like to read/watch contain which of the following elements?

    A. The fastest, most furious action

    B. Swords, sorcery, goblins, and dragons

    C. Mysterious mysteries

    D. Lightsabers and distant planets

    E. Crushes, sweethearts, and romance

    F. Tights, capes, and superpowers

What's your favorite kind of dessert?

    A. Doughnuts

    B. A freshly baked pie

    C. Crème brûlée

    D. Shaved ice (of any flavor)

    E. A box of fancy chocolates

    F. An ice cream cone (any flavor)

Which of these popular characters/actors in fiction do you identify with the most?

    A. The Rock (from any movies starring the Rock)

    B. Aragorn (from *The Lord of the Rings*)

    C. Sherlock Holmes

    D. Rey Skywalker

    E. Spider-Man (from *Spider-Man: Far From Home*)

    F. Thor

Your favorite class in school is:

A. PE

B. Art

C. English

D. Math

E. Theater

F. History

Now, count how many of each letter you circled. Then, take the letter you circled the most (if there is one) and look below to get a clue about how you may want to express your fandom. (But remember, you can ultimately choose any of these you want!)

A. *Naruto, Yo-kai Watch, BNA, Haikyu!!!*
   One Piece, Cells at Work!

B. *Fullmetal Alchemist, Little Witch Academia,*
   Ponyo, Children of the Sea

C. *Detective Conan, Young Miss Holmes, Spirited*
   Away, Mythical Detective Loki Ragnarok

D. *Last Exile, Doraemon, Carole & Tuesday,*
   Oban Star Racers, Mobile Suit Zeta Gundam

E. *Fruits Basket, A Silent Voice, Inuyasha,*
   Your Name., Mixed Vegetables, Yotsuba&!

F. *My Hero Academia, Cardcaptor Sakura,*
   Sailor Moon, Dragon Ball Z

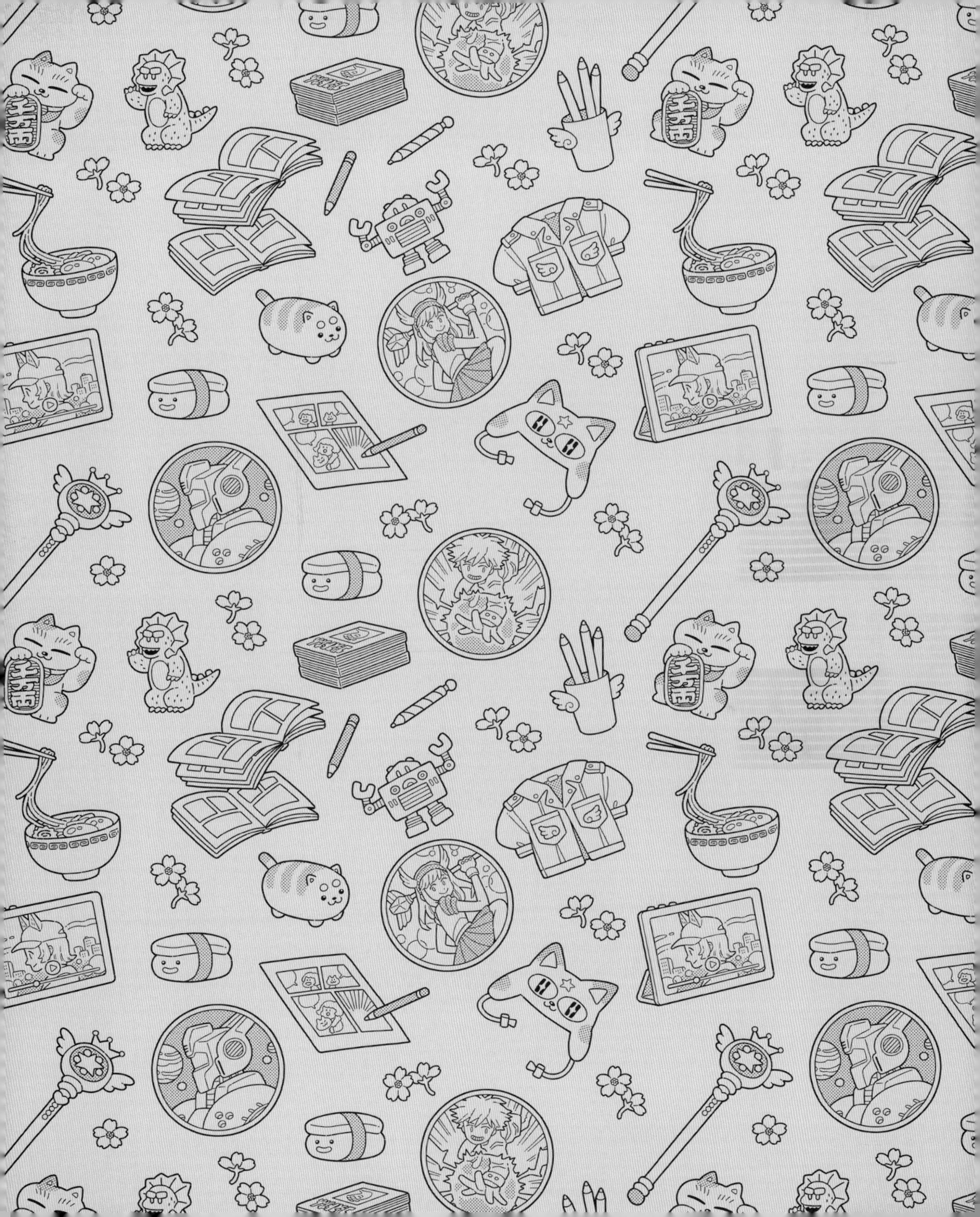

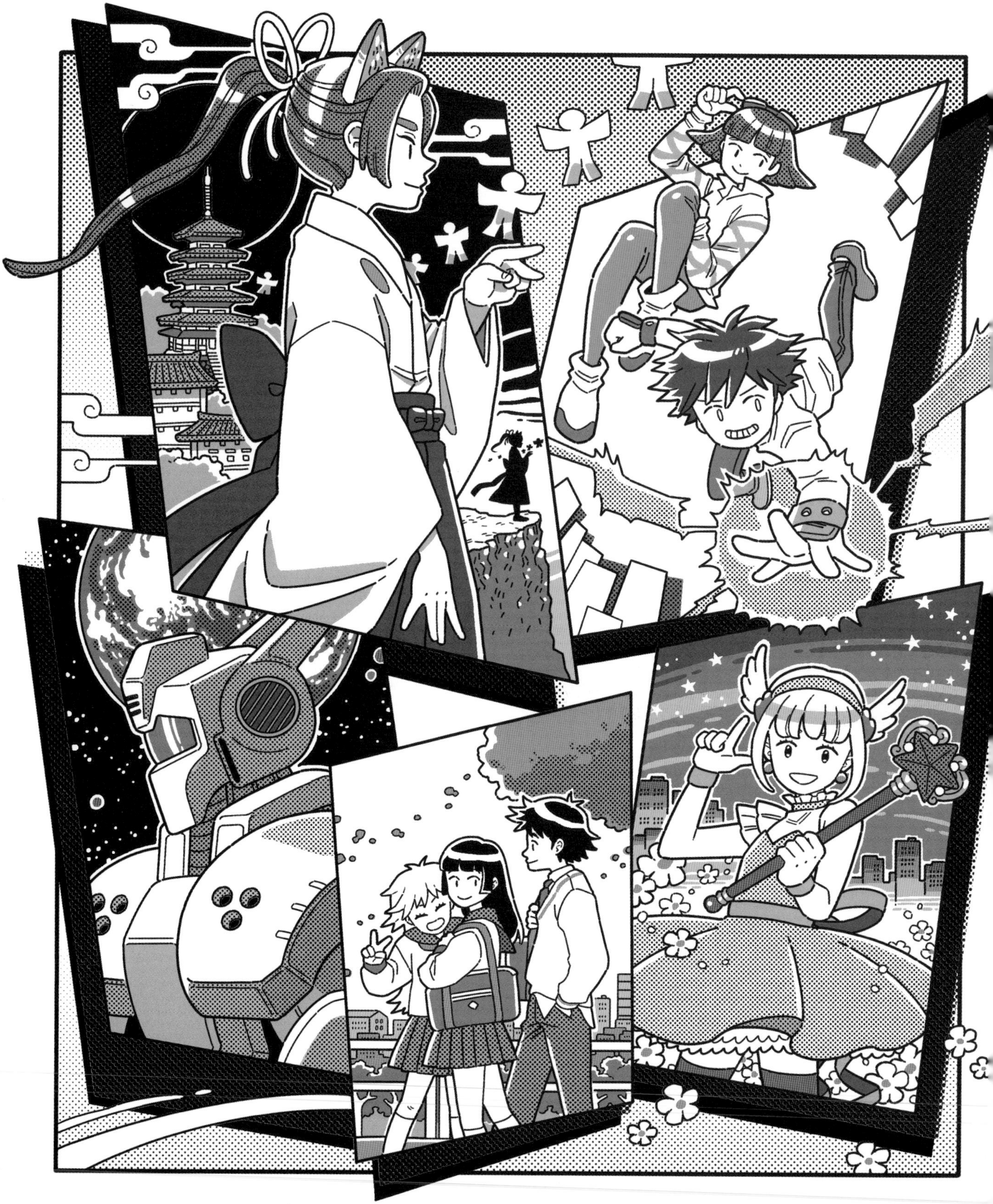

CHAPTER 4

SOMETHING FOR EVERYONE!

WHEN IT COMES TO ANIME and manga, things are a little different in Japan than they are in the United States. When you walk into a manga store in Japan, it's hard not to notice how many types of books there are. Not only are there manga for science fiction/fantasy, mystery, fiction, nonfiction, and much, much more, but also for different ages and genders, often in combination to create various subgroups. There seems to be manga published for just about anyone. While in the United States the categories for books are fewer and simpler, in Japan there's simply a much wider variety to choose from!

Don't be intimidated by all of these options! In fact, these manga and anime categories are easy to learn, and once you know more about them, you'll find picking the types of books, shows, and films you want to get into much simpler. The categories in manga and anime aren't there to confuse you, but instead to make reading and watching them an even better experience.

Let's begin with . . .

KIDS RULE THE WORLD!

Now we couldn't write this book without mentioning kids' manga, could we? And to be honest, a lot of what's in the **kodomomuke** ("for children" in Japanese) category is must-read material.

Pokémon might very well be one of the most popular kids' manga and anime on the planet, but those evolving beasties barely scratch the surface when it comes to stories created for younger audiences. In fact, some of the world's very first manga and anime were aimed toward young children, like *Anpanman*, *Doraemon*, *Cardcaptor Sakura*, and *Astro Boy*. Speaking of *Astro Boy*, the God of Manga himself Osamu Tezuka (read more about him in our manga chapter, page 44) created *so* much kids' manga that it solidified his reputation as the Walt Disney of Japan.

The stories in kids' manga and anime vary greatly, spanning different genres. From magical girls and sci-fi/fantasy to slice of life animal tales and, in the case of Detective Oshiri—who has a butt for a face—or Toriyama's *Dr. Slump*, silly comedy, kodomomuke has something for everyone and can be enjoyed by all ages.

SUGGESTED KODOMOMUKE SERIES

Yotsuba&!, *Chi's Sweet Home*, *Yoki Watch*, *Cowa!*, *Barakamon*, *Pui Pui Molcar*, *Little Witch Academia*, *Dinosaur Hour!*, *Cardcaptor Sakura*, *Doraemon*, *Hamtaro*

SUPER SHONEN!

Shonen simply means "boy" in Japanese. Now say the words *shonen anime* or *shonen manga*, and for fans some of the most popular and best-selling series of all time come to mind. *Dragon Ball Z*, *Naruto*, *One Piece*, and *My Hero Academia* are a few of the best examples of shonen anime and manga.

All of these hits began as serialized manga in the pages of *Shonen Jump* magazine, the biggest comic publication in Japan since 1968. Similar to how Marvel and DC Comics have their own unique style of storytelling, *Shonen Jump* specializes in tales about young heroes who overcome obstacles and that teach important values such as hard work, team spirit, and the power of self-improvement. Brought to life by talented artists and editors, shonen manga has had a winning formula for decades now, with no sign of slowing down.

Shonen Jump may have started out as a manga magazine for boys, but fans nowadays are all types of people from all over the world—anyone who loves the mix of drama, comedy, and action that shonen offers. And for slightly older fans, the category called **seinen** has similar thrills for young adults.

Jujutsu Kaisen and *Demon Slayer* are two of the most popular shonen anime out there—during the time we were writing this book—but you can bet there will be plenty more in the future. You just cannot beat that winning shonen spirit!

RECOMMENDED SHONEN SERIES

Fairy Tail, Bleach, YuYu Hakusho, Shaman King, Hunter x Hunter, Dr. Stone

ISEKAI-ANOTHER WORLD!

If you've ever seen an anime about an ordinary person who is whisked away to a far-off fantasy world full of excitement and adventure, then you've encountered what's known in Japan as an **isekai** story.

Isekai means "another world" or "a different world" in Japanese, and it's become a hugely popular concept in anime. Some anime fans credit the series *Sword Art Online* with kicking off the current isekai boom, but there have been similar series going back several decades into anime's past, such as *The Vision of Escaflowne* and *Magic Knight Rayearth*.

Modern isekai is deeply influenced by the popularity of video games and role-playing games. For instance, it's common for characters in isekai shows like *The Rising of the Shield Hero* to level up and gain new powers once they get experience points, which stems from these types of games.

Many isekai anime are based on a kind of book in Japan called a light novel. Some writers have come up with wild titles to get their anime noticed on the crowded shelves. That's why you'll sometimes find isekai anime with names such as *That Time I Got Reincarnated as a Slime* or *Do You Love Your Mom and Her Two-Hit Multi-Target Attacks?*

Either way, if you are a gamer, or just someone with a taste for fantasy tales, then there's plenty of isekai anime to enjoy!

RECOMMENDED ISEKAI SERIES

.hack//SIGN, Ascendance of a Bookworm, Digimon, Log Horizon, My Next Life as a Villainess: All Routes Lead to Doom

SUPER SHOJO!

Shojo is the Japanese word for "girl," and is one of the largest types of manga and anime. Aimed at teen girls, shojo manga usually focuses on romance, but sometimes with a genre spin—like in *Vampire Knight*, for instance, which combines romance, fantasy, and horror. And in the case of the well-known *Fruits Basket*, characters turn into members of the Chinese zodiac when hugged by the opposite sex. In *Cardcaptor Sakura*, the romance is mixed in with a magical girl adventure about a girl named Sakura who must find powerful cards to keep the world from being destroyed.

Much of shojo manga and anime lean toward slice of life, however, focusing on relationships and crushes. Many of these stories center on high school students and their relationships. Usually the main character is a girl, as in *From Me to You*, *Komi Can't Communicate*, and *House of the Sun*.

Although shojo manga is filled with wonderful stories, like josei manga, the plot can be a little mature, so you need to ask your parents first if you can read or watch these types of stories.

SUGGESTED SHOJO

Fruits Basket, Horimiya, Komi Can't Communicate, Orange, Nana, Ouran High School Host Club, Sailor Moon, Maid-Sama, Please Save My Earth, Love So Life, From Far Away

MECHA LOVE!

Where would anime be without giant robots—or **mecha**, as they are commonly called?

In many ways, mecha can be found just about everywhere! Battle bots like the ones seen in the anime series *Mazinger Z* and *Mobile Suit Gundam* are now modern symbols of Japan. Mecha anime has even inspired Hollywood blockbusters like *Pacific Rim* and *Transformers*.

While it's true that classic mecha series, such as *Voltron*, were originally designed to sell toys to children, mecha itself is not always kid stuff! For instance, the arty *Neon Genesis Evangelion* explores the warts-and-all inner lives of its young robot pilots. *Gurren Lagann* is a wild robotic comedy with surprisingly dramatic depth. And *Code Geass* tells an intriguing, complex tale of vengeance and betrayal.

It's important to keep in mind that not all mecha anime are about giant robots. Some mecha series, like *Bubblegum Crisis* and *Ghost in the Shell*, feature heroic robots and cyborg crime fighters who have human-sized adventures. But no matter how you look at it, if you want to know more about anime, sooner or later you'll want to "get in the robot!" and watch some shows about mecha.

RECOMMENDED MECHA SERIES

Gunbuster, Giant Robo, Eureka Seven, The Vision of Escaflowne, Macross, SSSS. Gridman, Magic Knight Rayearth

A SLICE OF LIFE!

While there are plenty of anime full of wild action and stories that stretch the imagination, sometimes you might find yourself needing a break from all the conflict and otherworld settings.

Slice of life anime is here for you like a hot bowl of chicken soup when you have a cold. Slice of life anime shares soothing stories about everyday things or heartfelt drama on a smaller scale.

Slice of life does not mean "boring," though! This category of anime can contain lots of comedy, romance, and even fantasy. Just don't expect intense scenes or big dramatic twists.

Instead, slice of life anime is more likely to show you cute characters doing cute things— like the schoolkids who start a band in *K-On!*—or good friends hanging out and enjoying each other's company—like the girls who love the great outdoors in *Laid-Back Camp*.

So take a break, slow down, kick back, leave your troubles behind, and enjoy some slice of life anime.

RECOMMENDED SLICE OF LIFE SERIES

Nichijou, Kaguya-sama: Love Is War, Anohana: The Flower We Saw That Day, Let's Make a Mug Too, Azumanga Daioh!, Barakamon, Silver Spoon

SPACESHIPS, SWORDS, AND SPOOKINESS!

Though not technically official categories of manga or anime, science fiction, fantasy, and horror make up so much of what you'll see out there, it's worth going into a few in detail!

Keep in mind that these books will span all the other categories we discuss, including shojo, shonen, kodomomuke, and seinen.

Manga and anime and science fiction have a long relationship, tracing back to characters like *Golden Bat* by Ichiro Suzuki in the 1930s and again to the post–World War II works of Osamu Tezuka, with *Nextworld*, *The Lost World*, and *Phoenix*.

Similarly, fantasy manga and anime have been around for a long time and may be the most popular genre in the medium today, with series like *Fullmetal Alchemist*, *Witch Hat Atelier*, and *Magic Knight Rayearth*.

Horror, which has been a theme in Japanese stories for centuries, became popular in early modern manga by creators like Kazuo Umezu in the 1960s and 1970s, with books like *Cat Eyed Boy*, *Orochi*, and *The Drifting Classroom*. Horror remains one of the most beloved genres to this day, led by the likes of Junji Ito.

A warning to our younger readers, however: some of these stories are geared toward older audiences, so you'll want to ask your parents whether a book or show or film is appropriate for your age before you read or watch it.

RECOMMENDED SCI-FI/FANTASY/HORROR SERIES

Nausicaä of the Valley of the Wind, XXXholic, Kaidan Restaurant, The Drifting Classroom, Escaflowne, A Certain Scientific Railgun, Inuyasha, Land of the Lustrous, Princess Tutu, Summer Wars, Ghost in the Shell, Battle Doll Angelic Layer

SPORTS! SPORTS! SPORTS!

While sports are a huge pastime around the world, did you know that they're also a hugely important and popular part of manga and anime?

Some of the medium's most popular stories have sports at their center, and perhaps it will come as no surprise that a lot of them are directed toward kids! From *Haikyu!!*, *Ace of the Diamond*, and *Slam Dunk* to *Real*, *Chihayafuru*, and *Blue Box*, **sports manga** spans various subject matter and even bleeds into other genres.

The stories in sports manga and anime are varied and don't always have to include athleticism. Though many revolve around popular sports like baseball, volleyball, swimming, and basketball, others concentrate on martial arts, mountain climbing, and even card games.

RECOMMENDED SPORTS SERIES

Yuri!!! on Ice, Sk8 the Infinity, Yowamushi Pedal, Be Blues!: Ai ni Nare, Baby Steps, H2, Initial D, Chihayafuru, The Prince of Tennis, Ping Pong, Ballroom e Youkoso, Hanebado

ADULT SUPERVISION REQUIRED

Seinen and **josei** manga and anime are aimed at adult men and women. Though *seinen* is translated from Japanese to mean "youth," the target audience is younger men, typically from eighteen to thirty years old. This is important to understand, since the themes and imagery in seinen manga and anime are typically darker and more violent. *Josei*—which simply means "woman" in Japanese—doesn't often contain darker themes, but these manga and anime are more focused on romance for adult readers ages eighteen and older.

There are many excellent seinen series to read or watch, but a word of warning: you should wait until you're older to interact with them, or if you want to watch them before you are a teenager, you'll need to ask a parent or caregiver. So, for now, concentrate on kodomomuke, shonen, and shojo. You can have a look at the maturer stuff in the future.

SUGGESTED SEINEN (FOR WHEN YOU ARE AN ADULT)

JoJo Bizarre Adventure, Cowboy Bebop, Attack on Titan, Serial Experiments Lain, Space Pirate Captain Harlock, Toradora!, KonoSuba: God's Blessing On This Wonderful World, Re:Zero: Starting Life in Another World

— ANIME FAN SPOTLIGHT —

INTERVIEW WITH DAWN H.

Dawn H. is the producer and host of the *Anime Nostalgia Podcast!* She started this podcast not only to talk about her love of older anime and manga, but also to share fandom history with younger fans and about how fandom has *always* been diverse. You can often find her writing for various places, rummaging for VHS tapes at local thrift stores, and posting photos of her cat on Twitter. Don't let her voice fool you: she's a lot older than she sounds.

What was the first anime you ever watched?

It's a little hard for me to remember exactly which was first, but the ones I remember vividly were the *Galaxy Express 999* movie, *The Fantastic Adventures of Unico*, *The Sea Prince & The Fire Child*, and reruns of things like *Astro Boy* and *Speed Racer*.

Where did you come up with the idea for the *Anime Nostalgia Podcast*? And what impact has it had on the anime community?

I was inspired to start up my own podcast by a few things. The first and major point being that I noticed most podcasts that were talking about anime were only talking about anime and manga that was coming out right at the moment. That's fun, of course, but there's so much older stuff that has kinda fallen away simply because fans who once loved them have moved on. I felt like a lot of older titles were worth remembering and talking about again, especially for younger generations who are newer to anime and manga who don't know they exist. Plus, it's fun to talk about fandom history and how much things have changed over the years. It also gives me an excuse to revisit older, more obscure titles to watch or read again and see if they really *are* worth remembering or not.

Another reason was simply that I was having a hard time finding anime and manga podcasts I actually liked listening to! When I started trying to listen to podcasts, I kept thinking, "Oh, if I were doing a podcast, I'd want to do it like this!" And I didn't really see myself in many of the podcast hosts out there. So I thought, "Why not just try it myself? It could be fun!" And I did. It was a learning experience, as I pretty much had to figure out what I was doing while I was doing it, but that was part of the fun!

I'm always proud to hear from people who say that they were inspired to start podcasting after listening to my show or started watching or reading a series because they heard me recommend something. I'm happy that the anime podcasting community continues to grow into a more diverse space, because that's what it's like in real life and has been for decades!

In this book, we discuss how anime and manga are more available than they used to be, particularly to people in the United States. Why do you think that is?

It's definitely more available than it used to be! I think the speed and ease of online streaming has helped things change a lot, as you used to only be able to get a select few anime as physical media or through the occasional airing of a few things on TV, and only a few publishers ever released manga in English. And since both anime and manga were considered niche media, they cost quite a lot to buy back in the day, and they were mostly sold via mail, comic book stores, or video stores. Now, you can buy anime and manga for much more affordable prices at *way* more places; there's more variety for a wide range of ages; and there's even lots of free and cheap ways to watch and read anime and manga! It's something that still impresses me, as someone who has lived through the eras where they were so expensive and a hassle to get.

What advice would you give kids who are looking to get into manga/anime—particularly the older anime you specialize in?

A great way to start is to think of what kind of genres you like in other entertainment you enjoy. Do you like reading fantasy novels? Or playing sci-fi video games? Then start by looking up fantasy anime or sci-fi anime, and see if there's anything that sparks your interest! Remember that anime is a medium, not a genre, so not all anime is going to appeal to you, just like not all movies or books or games will interest you. Talk to your friends and relatives that know what you like and see if they have any recommendations, too! Once you have a few titles in mind, you can also look up summaries or reviews online to see if they sound intriguing or just find out if you think the art looks cool. Keep an open mind, and you're sure to find things you'll be drawn to and fall in love with.

What are some of your favorite kids' anime and why? What did you grow up watching?

Some of my favorite kids' anime include:

- *Nausicaä of the Valley of the Wind:* The version I grew up with was famously edited really badly for its first American release, but even then it captured my imagination right away. Nausicaä is an amazing heroine with so much compassion for others. It was refreshing to see a "princess" who didn't look like what we usually envision when we hear that title!

- *Sailor Moon:* This series is so special to me because it came out when I was a little older than the characters, but still young enough to relate to many of their problems. It was so nice to have a series about all sorts of girls with different personalities and interests and with different strengths and weaknesses. It has so much heart and shows that there's no wrong way to be a girl—you can be strong *and* feminine if you want to!

- The Unico films: I grew up very attached to both of the Unico films for different reasons. The first one, *The Fantastic Adventures of Unico*, is a beautifully animated, charming adventure with cute characters and surprisingly high stakes. The second film, *Unico in the Island of Magic*, drew me in with its surreal weirdness, and I stand firm on my opinion that it's a children's horror movie.

- *Future Boy Conan*: While I didn't get to watch this series until much later in my life, I know that if I'd seen this series as a child, I would have absolutely loved it. The rich world-building, the likable characters, and the grand-scale adventure of this show are top-notch. The animation style is simple, but incredibly effective in how it's done. It's one of those shows I think an entire family can enjoy together.

What are your favorite anime and manga and why?

I have *many* favorites, but some of my older favorites include:

- *Maison Ikkoku*: While I'm a huge fan of pretty much all of Rumiko Takahashi's classic works, the *Maison Ikkoku* manga is probably my favorite. It's a story about love, loss, and growing up that I've been able to relate to at pretty much every stage of my adult life. It's funny, frustrating, heartbreaking, and heartwarming all at the same time. Takahashi is a master at creating characters that feel familiar and relatable and at putting them in some of the wackiest situations possible, and I feel like this is the strongest example of how amazing she is at character-driven narratives.

- *GoShogun: The Time Étranger*: A haunting and touching story about the bonds of friendship and what happens to heroes when they think they're done being heroes. I personally feel like it's an underrated gem and wish more people would give it a try!
- *Gunbuster*: A love letter not only to sci-fi and robot anime, but also to shojo anime, Hollywood movies, and other things the creators loved. From the incredibly detailed robot transformations and space battles to the heartbreaking character drama and uplifting victories, *Gunbuster* is a roller coaster of an **OVA** (original video animation) that is beautifully crafted. I cry watching the final episode. Every. Single. Time.
- *Dear Brother*: One of my favorite anime adaptations of Riyoko Ikeda's work directed by Osamu Dezaki, who is a *master* of limited animation. Every frame of this series looks like a beautiful, melancholy painting. Filled with sadness, angst, and teenagers making horrible decisions, it's no wonder that it was a huge influence on another big, over-the-top shojo hit I love: *Revolutionary Girl Utena*.

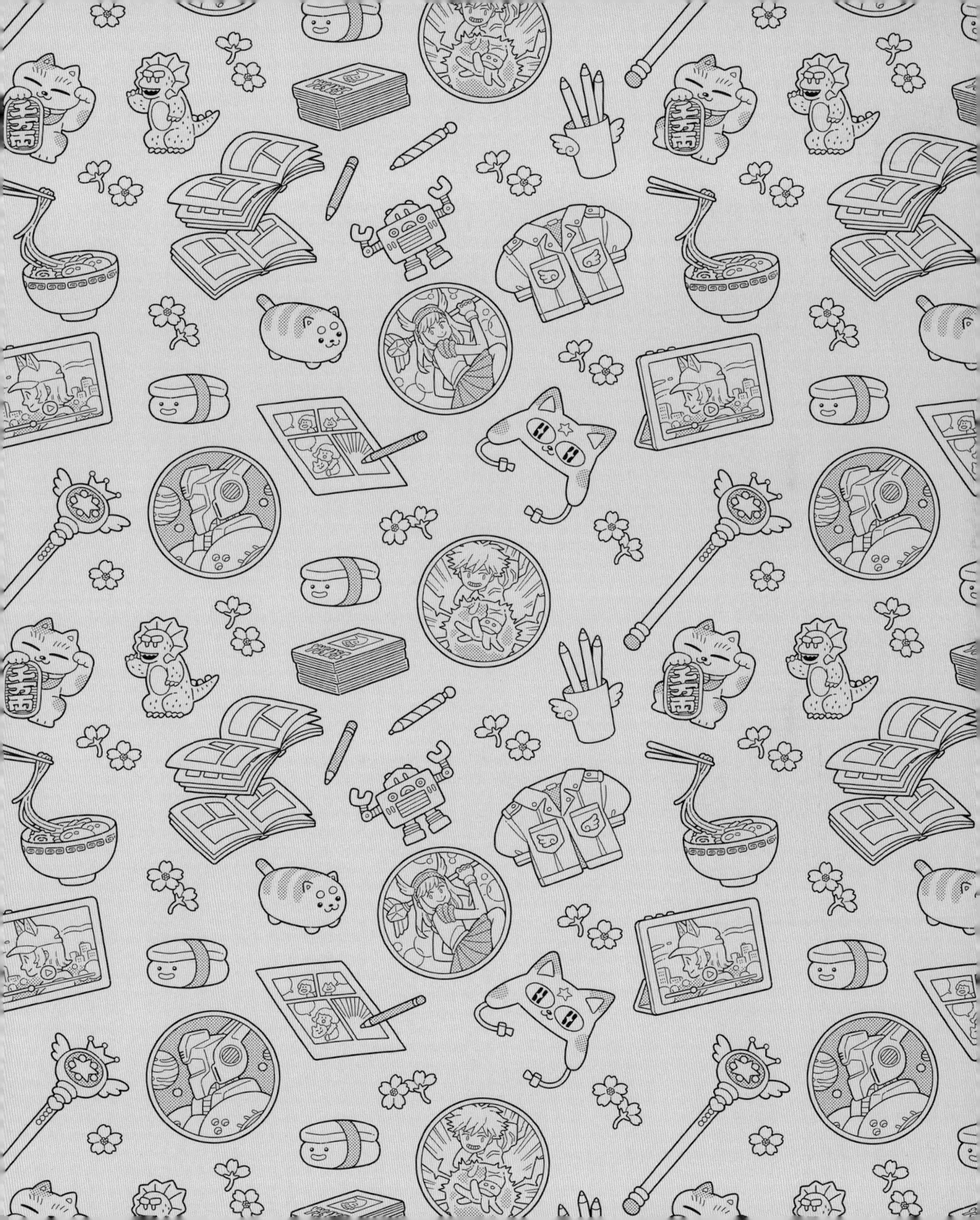

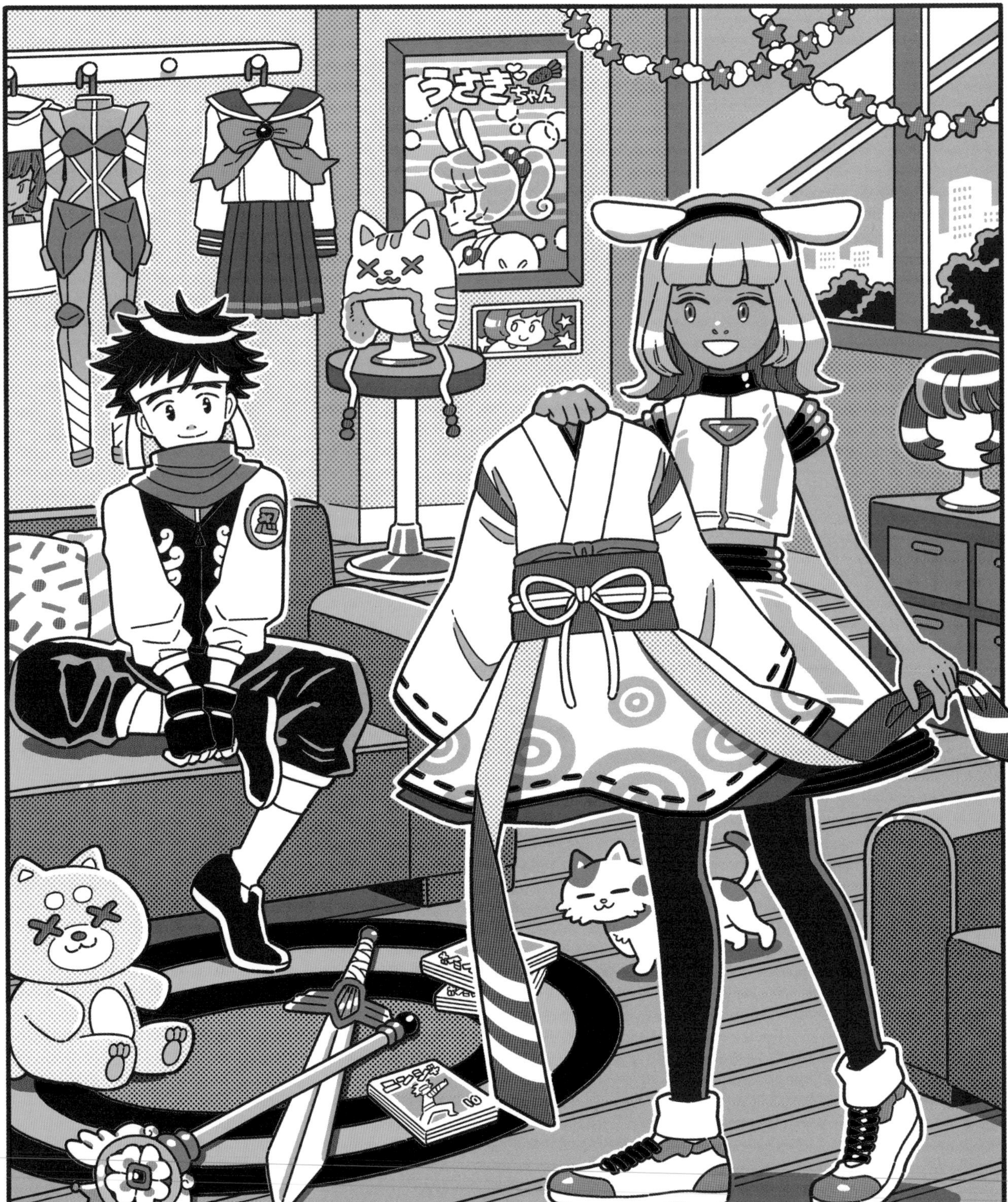

うさぎちゃん
忍
ニンジャ
10

CHAPTER 5

COSPLAY

IF **YOU HAVE EVER BEEN** to a convention with your parents or looked online to learn more about your favorite manga or anime, you've probably seen people dressed up like characters from shows and comics. Dressing up as a favorite character, whether from an anime, video game, manga, movie, or something else, is called **cosplay**—combining the words *costume* and *play*. One of the great things about cosplay is that no matter how fancy your costume is, it is all about sharing your excitement and love of your favorite characters and having fun!

Modern cosplay originated in Japan in the 1980s. As manga and anime grew in popularity there, fans began creating elaborate costumes and then showing off their work with other fans during conventions, meetup events, and through cosplay photography published in anime magazines.

Since then, cosplay has continued to grow in popularity all over the world, and it's hard to imagine what a large gathering of fans would be like today without people dressed as their favorite heroes and villains!

BUYING A COSPLAY COSTUME

In the early days of cosplay, fans had to make their costumes from scratch. But today, there are many companies that offer premade costumes, along with accessories like wigs and colored contact lenses so fans don't have to construct their cosplay looks if they don't want to.

Make sure you do your research first by reading reviews or getting a recommendation from a friend before you buy any costumes or accessories online. You want to make sure you are getting a good-quality premade costume that won't fall apart after a few wears.

You can also use a premade costume as a base, and then take it to the next level by getting it tailored for a better fit. (Ask your parents to help you find a place to get this done.) No matter if you make your own or buy your costume, always remember there are no true rules in cosplay. Just because you bought your costume off the rack instead of handcrafting it doesn't mean you can't look amazing—*and* have fun at the same time!

MAKING YOUR COSPLAY COSTUME

Starting out with a premade costume that you buy from a store or online is a good way to dip your toes into cosplay waters. But there might come a time when you'll want to level up by putting together a handmade costume. The basic tools and skills you'll need are the same ones that are key to any sort of clothing or accessory making. Be prepared to learn all about

fabrics and patterns, and if you or someone you know can operate a sewing machine, you'll be in good shape to start creating your own look!

Depending on who or what you want to dress up as, you might need some additional materials to bring that dream character or creature to life. For instance, foam is great for crafting things like armor and weapons, and you can create additional levels of dazzling detail using clay and other sculpting materials.

If you get stuck in your costume creation, no worries! There are lots of tutorials and videos online that can help you make your original costume a reality! And the more you practice making your own cosplay costume, the better you'll get, and the more confident you'll become.

HIRING SOMEONE TO MAKE YOUR COSTUME

In addition to buying a premade costume or making one from scratch yourself, there's another good option for people looking to get a quality cosplay look. You can order a costume from an experienced maker and pay someone to create an original outfit for you based on your size and preferences. Just search online for cosplay **commissions** or ask a friend with a fabulous outfit if they are interested in helping you make your cosplay dreams come true!

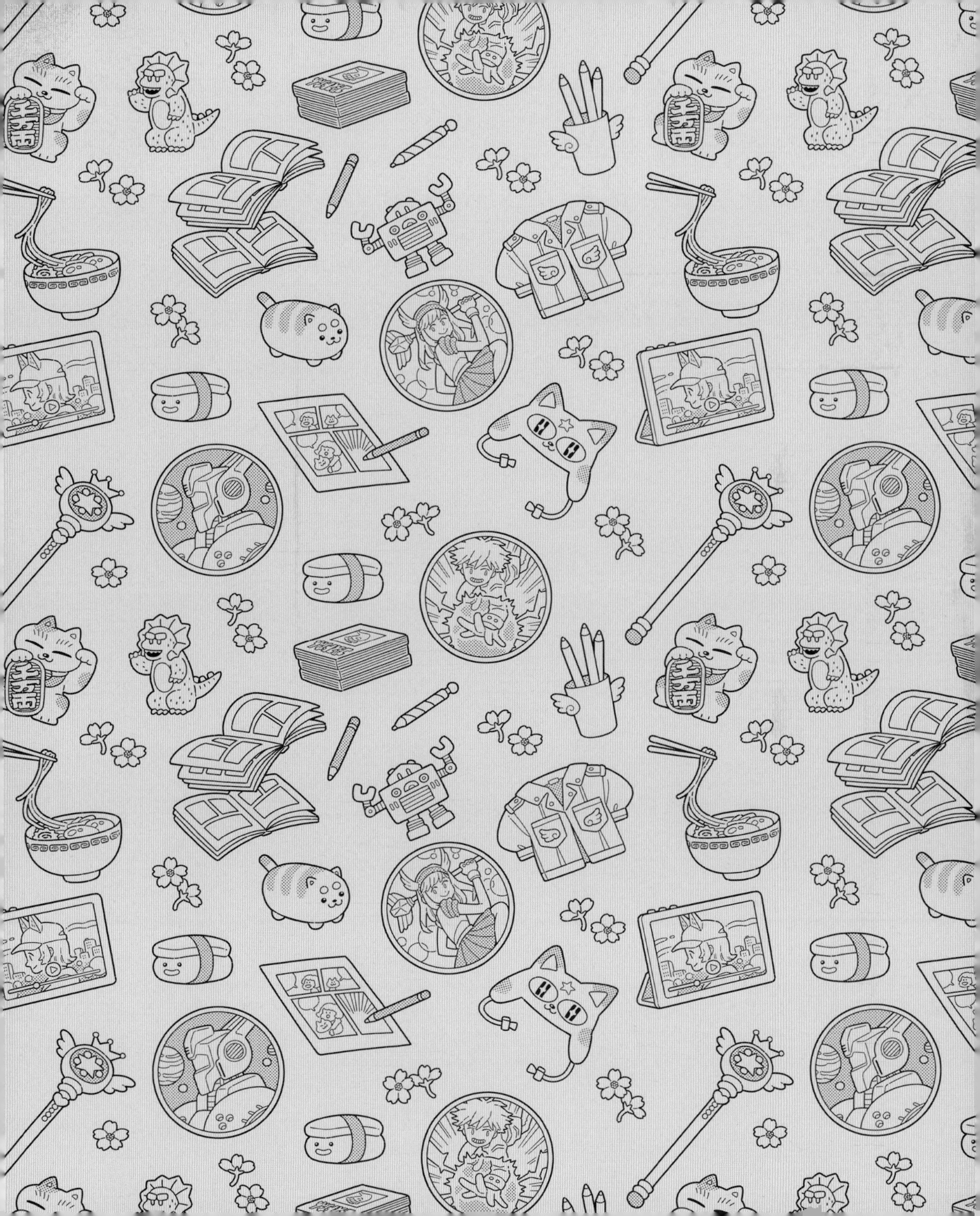

COSPLAYING AT CONVENTIONS!

You can do cosplay just about anywhere: in your room, at your friend's house, even at a public park! But sooner or later, you might want to go where the real action is and where lots of fellow cosplayers can be found— an anime convention!

We will talk more about anime conventions in Chapter 6, but here are a few tips for cosplayers who want to attend:

PLAN OUT YOUR COSPLAYS IN ADVANCE!

The more prepared you are, the more fun you'll have! You'll want to have every detail of your costume ready to go when the big day of the con finally arrives.

BE FRIENDLY!

You'll probably find lots of other cosplayers at the convention, maybe some even dressed as the same character as you! This is a great opportunity to have fun and make new friends who share your love of anime and manga.

BE PREPARED!

There is nothing more frustrating than spending all of your time getting your cosplay looking perfect and then a button comes off or part of your foam weapon starts to bend and break moments after you arrive at the convention or meetup. It is always a good idea to keep some double-sided tape or a thread and needle on hand just in case of a costume emergency.

COMPETITIVE COSPLAY!

The cosplay contest, or masquerade, is often a major highlight of anime conventions. This is where cosplayers take the stage, either as groups or alone, and show off their incredible costumes and props for everyone to see. Sometimes it's just for fun, but sometimes there are big prizes to win!

If you are interested in participating in a contest, you are first going to want to check the entry rules, so you know what the guidelines and expectations are. You don't want to wind up in the contest for advanced cosplayers if you're just a beginner!

Make sure you are in the right category for the contest, too. Some cosplay contests organize things by skill level, the quality of costume and prop construction, or even by acting ability—if cosplay skits are part of the program, that is.

Every cosplay contest is a bit different. Some judges give prizes based on the best performances, the best groups, the best craftsmanship, and so on. It's also common for cosplay contests to have special categories for younger cosplayers like yourself. Just be sure to look at the guidelines on any official website before you join. Finally, don't be nervous in front of the judges and crowd! Be proud of your costume, give it your all, and have fun!

COSPLAY PHOTOGRAPHY!

If you've put a lot of hard work into your cosplay costume, you should consider capturing the moment you are dressed and in character with cosplay photography! Cosplay photography can be anything from selfies with a cell phone to elaborate photo and video shoots worthy of a movie screen. It's entirely up to you how you want to capture this moment forever.

If you know a fellow cosplayer who has some great pictures, ask them to work with you on a photo shoot or to recommend a good, reliable photographer you can hire. (But ask a parent first, as this can be expensive!)

For your cosplay photo shoot, you have the chance to fully express your character, so make it a great performance, or just be silly and have fun. Again, the first rule of cosplay is: there are no rules!

COSPLAY IS FOR EVERYBODY!

In the end, cosplay is all about connecting with a character you love and bringing that character to life, even if it's just for a few hours or a couple of days at a convention. You certainly *don't have to* cosplay, but if you do, it's a great way to participate in fun activities, make friends, learn new skills, and build self-confidence. Think of cosplay as an exciting way to take your love of anime and manga to the next level!

MAKE YOUR OWN COSPLAY COSTUME

Making a manga/anime cosplay costume can be a bit of a challenge, especially if you haven't done it before. Hopefully the prompts below will help you get started and make this a little easier. Before you know it, you'll have your own special getup to wear at any cosplay gathering, whether with friends or at a convention. Now, let's begin!

What kind of theme/genre would you prefer?

    A. Sci-Fi

    B. Fantasy

    C. Horror

    D. Mystery

    E. Slice of Life

    F. Mecha

What kind of mood/feeling do you want your character to give off?

A. Strong (Goku, Izuku Midoriya, Ash Ketchum)

B. Funny (Monkey D. Luffy, Alphonse Elric, Chrome, Jiraiya)

C. Cute (Sakura Kinomoto, Anya in *SPY x FAMILY*, Rem in *Re:Zero*, Kiki, Ponyo)

D. Scary (Ryuk, Ken Kaneki, Team Rocket, No Face)

E. Romantic (Tuxedo Mask, Kraft Lawrence, Himiko Toga, Juvia Lockser)

F. Fantastical (Edward Elric, Saber, San/ Princess Mononoke, Mikasa Ackerman)

What tools, clothes, and weapons do you want your character to have?

A. Weapons: Sword, ax, staff, laser gun, lightsaber-like device

B. Head: Mask, hood, helmet, hat, elf ears, hair (or lack of), horns, wig

C. Body: Cloak, vest, dress, skirt, coat, armor (sci-fi or fantasy), uniform, holsters, bag and/or backpack, wings

D. Arms: Wraps, greaves (armor protecting the legs), gloves, bracelets or armlets

E. Legs/Shoes: Boots, tennis shoes, flats, leggings, pants

Now take your answers and start drawing a sketch of what your character looks like. You can try to create your own original character or choose one from a book to model on—recommended if you are first starting out. If you are modeling on an existing character, try to draw and/or write down each thing they are wearing!

After you're done sketching the different elements you'll need for your character, begin to work out what you'll need in order to create it! Talk to your parents about helping you through this part, since you might need their help with some of the sewing and gluing. NOTE: Remember to check your closet before you start making things, since you might have something perfect for your costume in there already—especially things like belts and boots. Some items may need to be purchased, such as a wig, for instance, and you can usually find inexpensive items like that online.

Next, think about downloading sewing patterns. A lot of costumes take some sewing to come together. Take a look at each part of the costume that you drew and try to find online sewing patterns to match. The sewing pattern will also recommend the kind of material you'll need. Remember again to ask your parents for help with this part, as you'll likely need someone to assist you in getting the fabric and, possibly, with the sewing itself.

After you have your sewing pattern, you're going to want to find some other important, flexible foamlike materials, especially if your character is wearing any armor or has any big swords or a helmet. Look into what are called thermoplastics, such as Wonderflex and Fosshape, which can be used to create a variety of metallic-looking items. Remember again to have your parents help you with this part, so that you make sure to get the right amount and colors that you need. For thermoplastics, you'll need a steam iron to shape the material. This is a simple procedure, but one for which you'll likely need to have a parent's supervision or help.

Other items you may require for crafting include:

- Glue/epoxy (parental supervision required)
- Heat gun (parental supervision required)
- Hobby knives (parental supervision required)
- Safety goggles
- Nitrile gloves
- Sewing machine (parental supervision required)

As you progress with making your costume, remember to create each piece separately. As you progress, you can see how your work is coming along and make changes as you go in order to get it to where you want it to be. Most importantly, the goal of making a cosplay costume is to have fun!

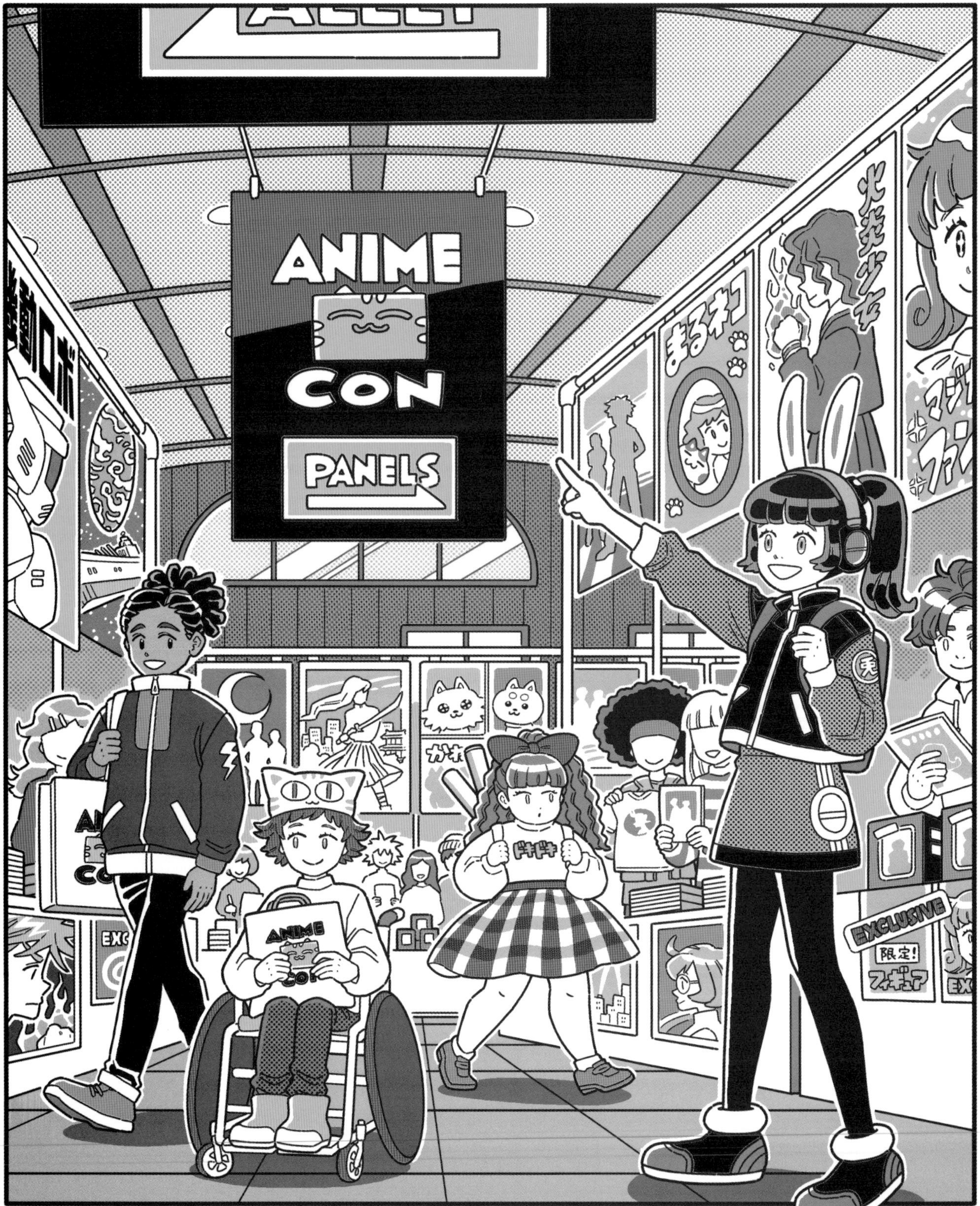
ANIME
CON
PANELS
光炎少女
まるネコ
ドキドキ
EXCLUSIVE
限定!
フィギュア

CHAPTER 6

COMICS, CONVENTIONS, AND FANDOMANIA!

IN THE PREVIOUS CHAPTERS, YOU'VE learned about the history of manga and anime, giving you a glimpse into the world that so many people love and are passionate about. Now it's time to talk about those special places where thousands gather to celebrate what they love and to build a sense of community with other anime and manga fans.

You may have heard about pop culture conventions before, and maybe you've even been lucky enough to attend one. Comic conventions, or comic cons, are the most well-known of these gatherings. San Diego Comic-Con is the largest in the United States. It takes place every year in July, and more than 100,000 people attend!

Many conventions in the United States and in other countries are focused on a wide variety of comics, television shows, and movies. While you'll probably find anime and manga at most conventions, there are some that are focused on anime only, such as Anime NYC and Sakura-Con.

It's important to know that you don't have to go to conventions to be a devoted anime fan or to be a part of the anime and manga fan community. But if you might be interested in learning more about conventions, this is the chapter for you!

THE RISE OF COMIKET

The first anime and manga convention was called Comiket, and it still takes place in Tokyo twice a year. It is the largest fan manga and anime convention in the world. This convention was first held on December 21, 1975, as a way for fans to meet up, share, and sell **doujinshi**. Though it might have started out with roughly 1,000 attendees, since then it has grown and grown. Now there are more than a million people who come to this convention each year. Comiket has in fact become two conventions split into two seasons, so fans attend either the Winter Comic Market in December or the Summer Comic Market in mid-August.

Unlike San Diego Comic-Con and other large conventions in the United States, Comiket is truly unique. The events still focus mainly on fan-made manga and comics, even though in recent years some larger companies have been able to set up booths to show and sell their products.

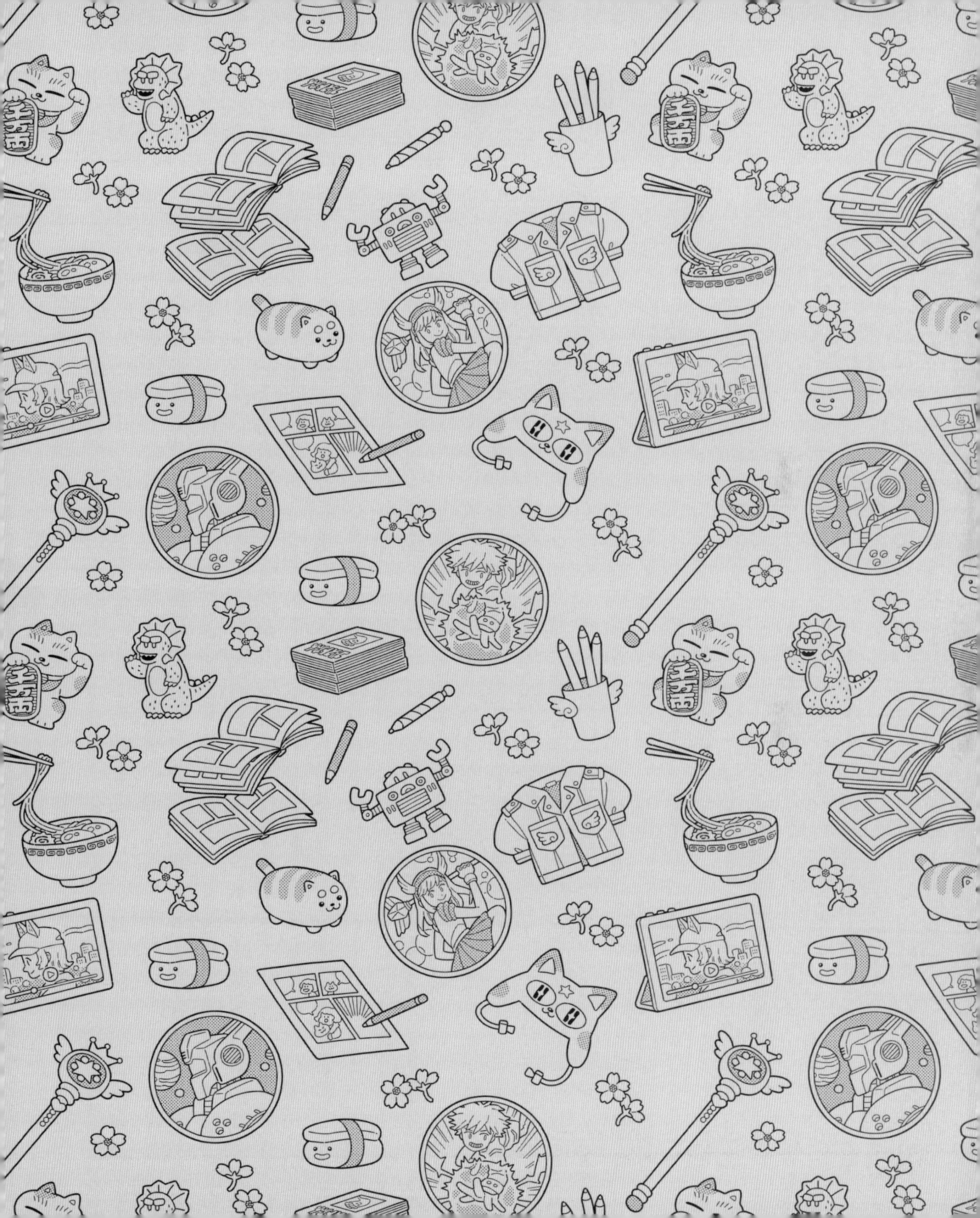

WHAT CAN YOU SEE AT AN ANIME CONVENTION?

CREATORS

From animators and illustrators to writers and game designers, anime and manga conventions always have many exciting guests. You can buy an art print from one of your favorite artists, listen to a talk from a famous animator, or even get a special **commission** created just for you!

DIRECTORS AND PRODUCERS

Directors and producers are also considered creators but are more concerned with the behind-the-scenes work of getting anime developed, sold, and animated/filmed. If you are interested in how anime is created and in how a film comes to be, you will want to visit a panel discussion with directors and producers. It's a great way to learn a thing or two about what brings anime to life.

VOICE ACTORS

Voice actors are perhaps one of the biggest draws at anime conventions, with fans gathering in large groups to get an autograph from the person behind the voice that brings their favorite character to life. The voice actors at these conventions come from all over the world. There are massive followings for English-speaking voice actors in particular, who hold events for autographs and photos at most of the major conventions.

COSPLAYERS

Cosplay is a massive part of pop culture conventions the world over, and anime and manga conventions are no exception. You'll be able to find designated spaces for cosplay at any anime and manga convention, whether you are participating in it or you simply want to see some cool costumes!

You can read more about cosplay in Chapter 5.

COSPLAY COMPETITIONS

Though you should refer to Chapter 5 on cosplay for more information about specific competitions, it's good to know that you can often find these exciting events at conventions! From Anime Expo to Comiket, cosplay competitions are a huge part of what brings fan communities together at large events like these.

MUSICIANS

Music is a major part of any anime convention because music is a massive part of anime itself! As you watch more anime series and films, you'll soon have your own favorite theme songs and soundtracks. Many of the Japanese bands that play music for anime are incredibly famous in Japan as well, so seeing them in person at a convention can be an electrifying fan experience.

PANELS

Want to learn about rare Pokémon, dive into *JoJo's Bizarre Adventure* lore, or listen to various voice actors, writers, and artists talk about what they love most about their work? Then panels are where you need to head at a convention. There are hundreds of panels you can attend at an anime convention. Some are so packed you'll have to line up early to get in, so make sure to plan in advance so you don't miss the one you really want to go to!

WORKSHOPS

Anime conventions provide interesting workshops where you can learn anything from leathercraft and prop-making (to add on to your cosplay costume) to taiko drumming and **Gunpla**.

SCREENINGS

One of the exciting things about attending an anime convention is getting access to early screenings for new trailers, shorts, **AMVs** (which are a type of anime music video), and even new episodes or films of favorite anime or brand-new series.

CONCERTS

Sometimes anime conventions might have a large concert as part of the program, with many different performers sharing the stage, including bands with songs that appear in anime as well as DJs. In some cases, there are even full classical music performances where the musicians play instrumental scores from popular Ghibli or other films.

ARTIST ALLEY

An anime convention wouldn't be complete without an artist alley. This is where artists display their original work and prints to purchase at booths. Convention attendees can come through and buy the artwork directly from the illustrators. This is often one of the most dynamic and exciting locations at anime conventions.

ANIME EXPO—
LOS ANGELES, CALIFORNIA

Held during the first weekend of July, Anime Expo is one of the most popular conventions in the world, hosting over 100,000 attendees and featuring a variety of famous guests and events.

FANIMECON—
SAN JOSE, CALIFORNIA

One of the oldest anime conventions in the United States, FanimeCon is smaller than Anime Expo, but it offers just as much action, including AMV competitions, screenings of new shows, karaoke, and a vibrant artist alley.

A-KON—
IRVING, TEXAS

A-Kon is North America's longest-running anime convention, debuting in 1990. Mostly staffed by volunteers, this midsize convention continues to draw about 34,000 attendees per

JAPAN EXPO
PARIS, FRANCE

The largest anime and manga convention outside of Japan, the Japan Expo boasts over 240,000 attendees each year. Japan Expo attracts a variety of events and guest appearances from famed anime producers, artists, and mangaka.

MANGA BARCELONA
BARCELONA, SPAIN

Beginning in 1995 and held every year since, Manga Barcelona is Spain's largest anime convention. It hosts a variety of events, including the World Cosplay Summit, anime conferences, and workshops, and offers various kinds of Japanese cuisine for attendees.

COMIKET
TOKYO, JAPAN

As previously discussed in this chapter, Comiket is the world's first anime and manga convention, drawing more than 500,000 attendees. The convention takes place twice a year—summer and winter—and focuses mainly on doujinshi, or fan comics.

CLOSING TIME . . .

Conventions are a big part of what makes anime and manga thrive and continue to grow. Though the first ones began small, with just a few hundred attendees, these conventions quickly became a place for fan communities to gather and share their mutual love of anime and manga. Whether you're coming to a convention to collect art, meet a favorite voice actor, listen to music, learn about the anime industry, or watch cosplay competitions or participate in them yourself, you'll be greeted warmly and enthusiastically by others who feel the exact same way you do about anime and manga.

CONVENTION CHECKLIST!

If you're heading to a convention, it's a good idea to do some planning. Here are a few things that are key to enjoying a convention and being safe.

- ☐ A backpack
- ☐ Water bottle
- ☐ Plenty of snacks, as it isn't always easy to find food
- ☐ An extra battery or charging cord to keep your phone charged
- ☐ Comfortable clothes—especially walking shoes, since you'll easily be walking miles
- ☐ Toiletries, like a toothbrush/toothpaste and deodorant, because you never know when you'll want to freshen up
- ☐ Quick-fix supplies, including glue, tape, extra foam material, makeup, hair product, and a pocket mirror
- ☐ Cash
- ☐ Hand sanitizer, to keep yourself from coming home with **con crud**
- ☐ Sharpies, so you can get an impromptu autograph from a guest star you notice in passing

YOUR PARENTS ARE COOL!

That's right, we said it. Your parents are cool. And since attending a convention is something you won't want to do alone as a kid, you should talk to your parents about ways to put together a safe, fun, and organized visit. Your parents might even be anime and manga fans themselves, which means they can probably help you plot out a convention plan that everyone can enjoy.

BRINGING FANDOM HOME!

It's important to remember that you don't need to go to a big convention to celebrate your fandom. There are lots of local ways you can get involved, from organizing a club at school with your friends to asking the school library to help host a convention for the kids at your school. A little creativity goes a long way. And who knows, you might even create something entirely new!

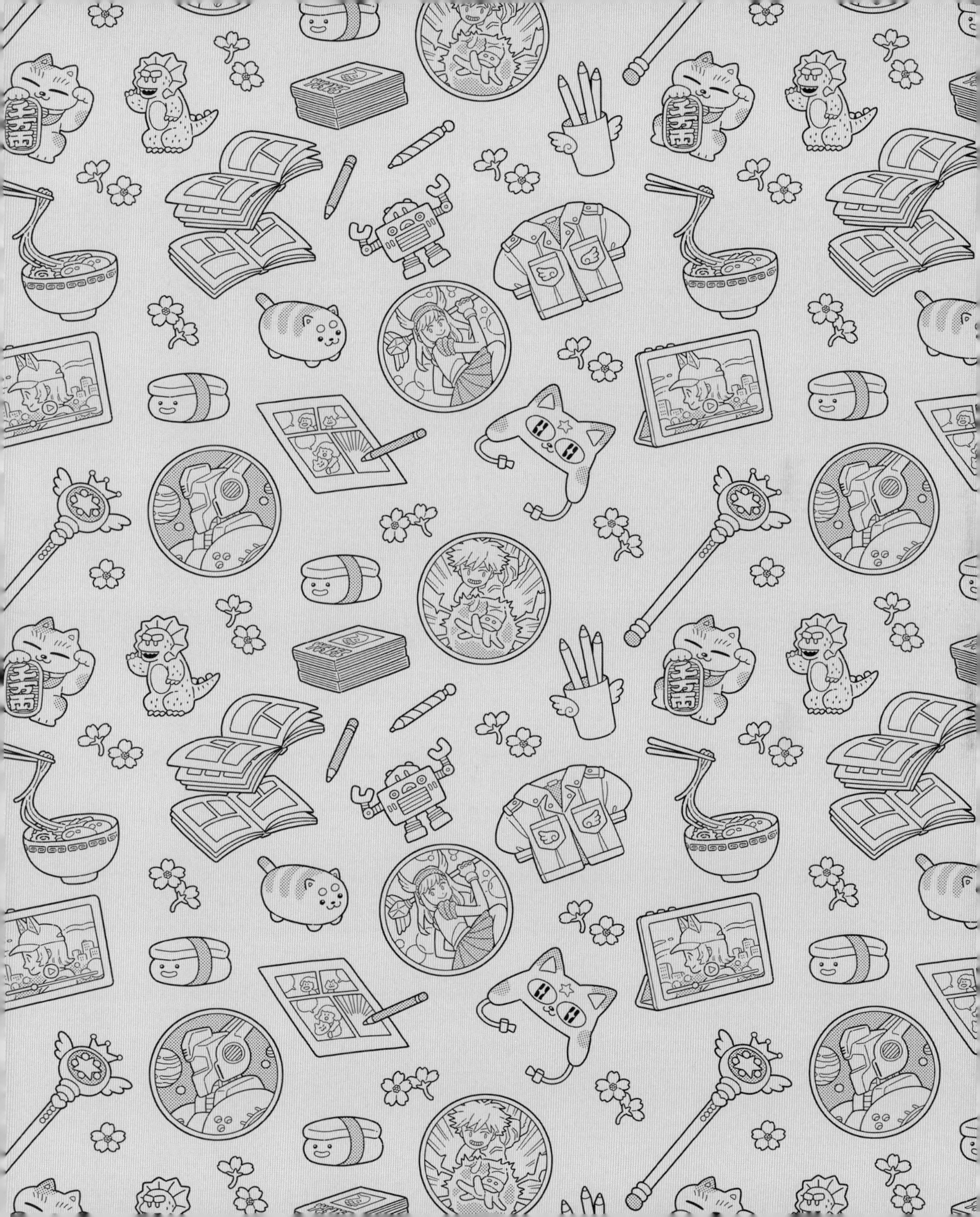

— VOICE ACTOR SPOTLIGHT —

INTERVIEW WITH DENEEN MELODY

As a child, Deneen Melody was known for her wild imagination and performance flair, often obsessing over fantasy films, anime, and video games. While she trained and performed as a ballerina till her early twenties, an injury caused her to move away from the world of dance and into the world of acting. Deneen's voice can now be heard in a variety of projects, including the Rebuild of Evangelion films, *Sword Art Online*, *Genshin Impact*, *Rainbow High*, and *Miraculous: Tales of Ladybug & Cat Noir*.

What was the first anime you ever watched?

> I have the most vivid memories of watching the Unico films as a small child. My family was very much into anime during the 1980s and early '90s, so while I know I watched a few different things early on, Unico is the one that has stuck with me. It's honestly everything I love! Cute and magical, but also surreal and *really* disturbing. Little me loved that!

When did you start doing voice acting for anime? Can you describe how you got into that?

I booked my very first anime role in 2018. After wanting to be in anime for years, I decided to finally go for it and started taking my first set of classes with Adventures in Voice Acting. After attending a variety of classes and dubbing workshops, I eventually had the opportunity to read for Mami Okada, the casting director for Bang Zoom! Studios in Burbank, California. After a few months, she cast me as my first character, and I've been working in anime ever since!

How do you get into character when preparing to do voice acting for an anime role?

It depends! There are times I may be cast in a role and have *no idea* who or what the character is. I won't even know till I'm in the booth and have to record. When that happens, I trust the director to guide me and we'll find the character together. However, the great thing about anime is that it may already be available to watch in Japanese, there could be an existing manga, or I can find information online. If I know my character beforehand and any of these resources are available, it is a huge help!

Who are some of your favorite anime characters? Have any of them inspired the character roles you've filled in your voice acting career?

Hitomi Kanzaki and Allen Schezar from *The Vision of Escaflowne*, Aisha from *Outlaw Star*, Reiner Braun from *Attack on Titan*, Lain from *Serial Experiments Lain*, and Asuka from *Evangelion* are just a few of my favorite characters. (Believe me, I have many!) Hitomi is the type of character I have always wanted to play, and she has provided inspiration toward some of my own roles. Same with Aisha. I voice quite a few characters with dynamic personalities, and my mind will automatically think of Aisha whenever these characters pop up. Then, we have Asuka, who means a lot to me on a personal level. Feeling such a connection to her after all these years really helped my performance as

Mari in the Evangelion films. It was easy to be Mari opposite her. I just felt like I truly knew Asuka in those moments.

In this book, we discuss how anime and manga are more available than they used to be, particularly to people in the United States. Why do you think that is?

Well, with the help of the internet over the years, I believe more and more people have become aware of how awesome anime and manga are! There is a large demand for them all over the world now, not just in Japan, and fans are incredibly passionate. I mean, take a look at the number of anime conventions in the United States alone! It's incredible!

What advice would you give kids who are looking to get into manga/anime? Where should they start?

I can only speak for the voice acting side, but . . . classes. I always, always recommend classes. Whether you would like to do voice acting as a hobby or pursue it as a professional career, there is so much more to it than being able to do a bunch of voices. Also, it's okay if you are unable to take classes at first. Just watch more anime! Before I took my first class, I would watch anime with the subtitles, mute it, and act out the scenes myself. I did this with video games as well. It may seem silly, but it's a great way to practice and build confidence. (Maybe even get a couple of friends to join you!)

What is your favorite anime and why?

The Vision of Escaflowne. To this day, it is still the most beautiful anime I have ever seen. In fact, every time I rewatch it, I cannot get over how beautiful it is. I'm also emotionally invested in *Neon Genesis Evangelion*. I was around the same age as the Eva pilots when I first watched it, and I felt for them. (I could never blame Shinji for not wanting to pilot the Eva!) Lastly, I want to mention a newer anime called *Dance Dance Danseur*. Before becoming an actor, I was a professionally trained ballet dancer, so I know and understand the world of *Dance Dance Danseur* quite well! Watching it brings back so many memories.

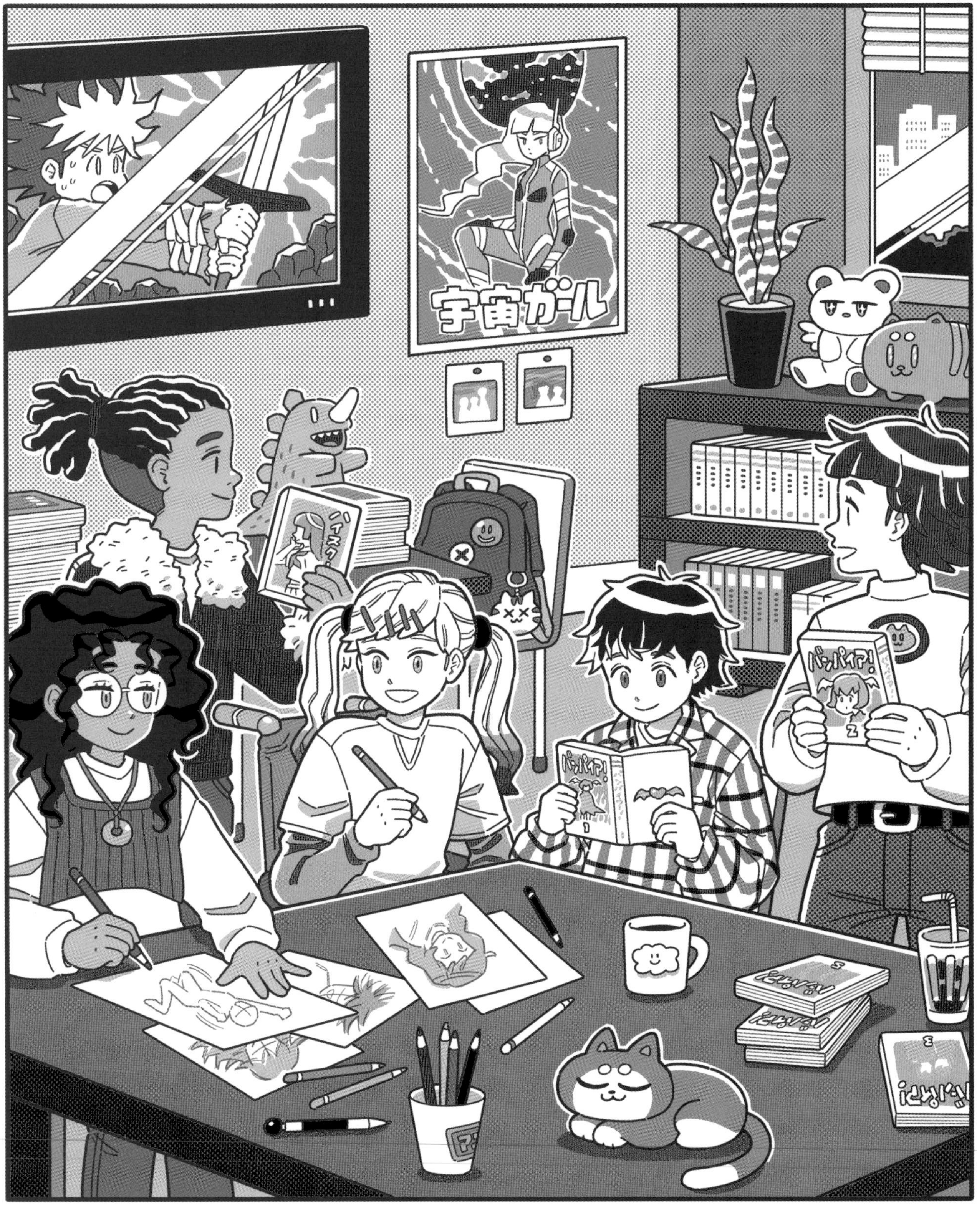
宇宙ガール
バンパイア!
バンパイア!

CHAPTER 7

GETTING INVOLVED WITH ANIME AND MANGA

THE MAGIC OF ANIME AND manga comes from how they enter your life and stimulate your imagination. The memorable characters and incredible settings in the series you love can help you enter another universe . . . or just see your own life from a different perspective!

For some fans, it's enough to simply enjoy anime and manga as entertainment only. But for fans who want to go deeper, an interest in anime and manga can open whole new worlds of creativity and even develop new skills. And if you choose to express yourself in a field related to anime and manga—as the authors of this book did!—you might just find yourself becoming something of a creator as well!

FAN ART!

Sooner or later, it seems like every fan tries drawing their favorite characters from their favorite anime and manga. And why not? It's easy! All you need to get started in fan art is some paper and simple drawing tools like pencils or pens. People also use digital tablets to sketch and create their illustrations, but don't feel like you need anything complex to enjoy making fan art.

One good way to learn about the unique art styles used in anime and manga is to try copying some of your favorite art. Take a page or a panel from a manga that appeals to you. Note how the lines have been put together to create certain effects like texture and shading. Try to get a sense of how the artist makes the characters pop or what techniques were used to bring the action to life.

Copying is a good way to start learning the basics of anime and manga art, but you probably shouldn't do it forever. Be bold and try drawing your favorite characters the way only you can imagine them, or better yet—why not try to create your own original characters?

Don't worry if your art isn't perfect. Even the greatest anime and manga artists are not always happy with their work! What matters is putting in the time and trying to improve your skills. You'll soon find that making art is like most things in life: the more you do it, the better you'll get.

FAN FICTION!

Anime and manga are such visually striking mediums that sometimes it's easy to ignore the power of the words in these shows and books. What would your favorite stories be like without the memorable lines of dialogue, the strong character voices, or the world-building that go into the telling of works like *My Hero Academia* or *Demon Slayer*?

In truth, writing is the backbone of many great anime and manga, and the good news is, it's easy to have some fun creating your own stories and characters by sitting down with a notebook or laptop and letting your imagination run wild.

From experience, I can tell you that writing about anime helped turn me into a professional author. Growing up, I was so impressed by anime like *Space Battleship Yamato* and *Robot Carnival* that I tried writing about what I saw on the screen just for fun. I found out that I enjoyed writing and kept on doing it, and here I am now, cowriting this book!

Writing stories inspired by anime and manga is known as fan fiction, and there are no rules on what you can or can't write. While I wrote about what I saw on-screen, like a novelization, there are plenty of people who create new stories based on their favorite anime and manga. For example, ever wonder what your favorite characters did in between the episodes you watched? Write about it! Ever wonder what might happen after the final chapter or episode of your favorite series? Create it! How about a crossover between epic characters like Luffy from *One Piece* and Naruto? Well, why not imagine it and then write your own story?

Once you have come up with a story you're happy with, you can share it with a massive community of online fan fiction creators for feedback or you can just keep it to yourself. Either way, expressing your love of anime and manga through writing is a great way to explore your own creativity and to increase your connection to fandom.

REVIEWING!

Fan fiction isn't the only way to write about anime and manga, though. Reviewing series, films, and manga is another great way to express yourself and develop some writing and critical thinking skills along the way.

Reviewing anime or manga is simple to do: watch some anime or read some manga; then write down your thoughts and feelings about it! Do you think the story worked as well as it could have, or could the creator have done something different to make it even better? Did the characters seem interesting or was something lacking that kept you from really caring about them? Were there any highlights or dramatic moments you'd want to tell someone about (without spoiling the story, of course!)? How did this film or series compare with similar stories that came before it in the same genre? You're the reviewer, so you get to decide!

ANIME CLUBS!

If you are looking to connect and hang out with other anime and manga fans in person, then seeking out an anime club in your neighborhood or school might be a good idea—but, of course, always tell your parents if you are joining a club set outside of your home.

There are all kinds of anime clubs, ranging from ones where fans meet to watch and discuss classic titles and the latest releases to clubs that offer fun activities like cosplay, drawing, and even karaoke!

Anime clubs can often be found at public libraries or on school campuses. Search online for an anime club near you or ask your fellow fans or trusted adults if they know of any in your area. You might just find yourself with a whole new circle of friends who share your favorite hobby.

LEARNING JAPANESE!

Make no mistake about it: anime and manga are a great introduction to Japanese culture. If you're the sort of person who becomes interested in the language that your favorite series was first created in, then learning a bit of Japanese can help bring you deeper into your favorite anime and manga.

If you live in a big city, you might find Japanese classes taught at a local school or in a nearby Japanese community center. Ask a parent or teacher to help you search online to see what's available near you.

If you are the sort of person who prefers to learn on your own, there are a lot of free resources online, including lessons from sites like NHK.org and video vocabulary drills on YouTube.

The main thing is to keep studying and to try to keep on learning no matter what path you take: classes, self-study, or online tutoring. And if you want a break from studying, then just pop on some anime. You might even pick up some new words or phrases without even knowing it!

MAKING YOUR OWN ANIME OR MANGA!

For some fans, this is it—the final frontier, the ultimate dream: making their very own manga or anime and sharing it with the world.

This is not as unrealistic as it might seem at first. Many top creators, both in Japan and around the world, started out by making their own comics. And as digital tools become more available, it's possible to set up original animation at a level of quality that was unthinkable a few years ago.

If you choose to tell stories using manga, you can upload your finished work to sites like Webtoons or Manga Plus Creators and try to build your audience as best you can through regular story updates and engaging with your readers. You might just wind up with a hit series—anything is possible!

Making your own anime requires some next-level skills and hard work, along with computer power, to bring those dreams to life. Most independently produced anime is made with digital technology. Tools that the pros use, like Clip Studio Paint, are available for anyone to buy, and tutorials for how to use them can be found online.

Making animation might seem like a huge task, but start small and play around. In the case of a hit indie-animation series like *RWBY*, the American creators were inspired by their love of anime to create their own show, improving the quality of production as their skills and audience grew. Now, *RWBY* is getting an official anime spin-off made in Japan.

Keep in mind that making your own manga or anime is hard work and a long road with no guarantee of success. But don't let anyone tell you that it's impossible, because if you are passionate about anime and manga, you are already ahead of the game!

— REVIEWER SPOTLIGHT —

INTERVIEW WITH KARA DENNISON

Kara Dennison is a writer and editor who has worked with Crunchyroll, *Otaku USA Magazine*, *Sci-Fi Magazine*, Fanbyte, and many other publications, writing about anime and other pop culture topics. In addition, she's the author of several novels and short stories, with more always on the way. In her spare time, she enjoys tabletop gaming and looking after her guinea pigs.

What was the first anime you ever watched? What was the first manga you ever read?

I was watching anime at a very early age without even realizing it! The first anime I remember watching were the two Unico films. I loved those so much, I made my own little cardboard cutout Unico to carry around with me since I couldn't find a stuffed animal.

I didn't read any manga until college, even though I'd gotten more into anime over the years. Our college anime club read *Vampire Princess Miyu* together—someone would print out the pages on clear sheets and show them on an overhead projector, and we'd read from a printed-out translation like we were doing a radio play. The first manga I read on my own, though, was *Inuyasha* about a year before the anime started. Back then, the U.S. releases would still flip the pages to read like American comics.

When did you start writing about anime? Can you describe how you got into doing that?

My first big job after college was at a news website, and I did that for almost ten years. I was around for a lot of big changes, like news websites using social media to get their stories out. After that, I worked as a subtitle editor for a few anime and game companies, including Crunchyroll and Discotek. That was a lot of fun because I got to see shows I might not have watched otherwise; also, I got to help get classic shows like *Mazinger Z* in front of more people!

I was approached to join the Crunchyroll News team a couple of years later when they were looking to add more people. Around the same time, I was asked to write a piece for *Otaku USA* because I knew a lot about a very specific genre of anime they wanted to feature. I've written for a lot of different places since then, and everyone gets into it differently. In my case, I think it had a lot to do with how much time I had spent as a journalist, in addition to my anime knowledge. Getting to combine the two things is really exciting!

In this book, we discuss how anime and manga are more available than they used to be, particularly to people in the United States. Why do you think that is?

There are a lot of things that happened around the same time to make anime and manga more available than they once were. Entertainment in general is a lot easier to get, for one thing. For another, anime fans like us decided they wanted to use their skills to make anime more accessible to everyone!

It's thanks to a lot of people who grew up loving anime and wanting better access to it that we have anime and manga coming out translated into English at the same time it is released in Japan! And it's because people care about older shows that we're getting classic anime and manga decades later. Twenty years ago, we never dreamed we'd have it this good.

What advice would you give kids who are looking to get into manga/anime? Where should they start?

The big thing to remember is that anime and manga aren't a genre. There are lots of genres in anime and manga, and the trick is to find something you already like. That's how I've gotten friends of all ages to give different anime and manga a try.

In terms of recommendations, Studio Ghibli films are a great place to start. I recommend *My Neighbor Totoro* and *Kiki's Delivery Service* especially. There's a reason they're classics: no matter where you're from or where you grew up, you'll find something you relate to. Best of all, you can watch them with your family.

What about for people who are interested in writing about manga/anime? What advice would you give?

My advice for writing about manga and anime is the same advice I have for writing about anything: read a lot and write a lot!

Read as much as you can, and as you read, ask yourself what you like or dislike about what you're reading. That's a great way to start figuring out how to improve your own writing, as well as what you'd like to see more of.

Always practice writing, even if no one else ever sees it. The more you write, the better you'll get.

Most of all, try to expand your horizons. You don't have to know every series. But if you know what genre you like, watch as much as you can within it, and learn about its history. For me, that's magical girls and giant robots. All anime and manga these days are made by people who grew up loving anime and manga themselves. So the more you know about what came before, the more you'll be able to say about what comes next!

What are some of your favorite kids' anime and why? What did you grow up watching?

I grew up watching mostly what came out on Nickelodeon, back when I didn't know what anime was. *Grimm's Fairy Tale Theater* was one I loved a lot. Then *Sailor Moon* came out, and I was a big fan of that, of course!

Nowadays, I love watching every new season of *Pretty Cure* as it comes out. My best friend also got me interested in *Digimon* recently, so I've been giving a few seasons of that a try.

What is your favorite anime/manga and why?

I love magical girls and giant robots, but my go-to anime series is *Lupin the Third*. I saw *The Castle of Cagliostro* in college, and it was the first time an anime really amazed me and made me fall in love with everything anime can be. I told my friend who showed it to me, "It's so sad this is only one movie. I'll never see these characters in anything else again" . . . not realizing how much Lupin there is!

As a fan of all different eras of anime, I love how Lupin has changed and grown over the years. Each different era is unique and has movies and series made by great creators of the time. Plus, I'm a big fan of heist and adventure stories that are just a little bit fantastical.

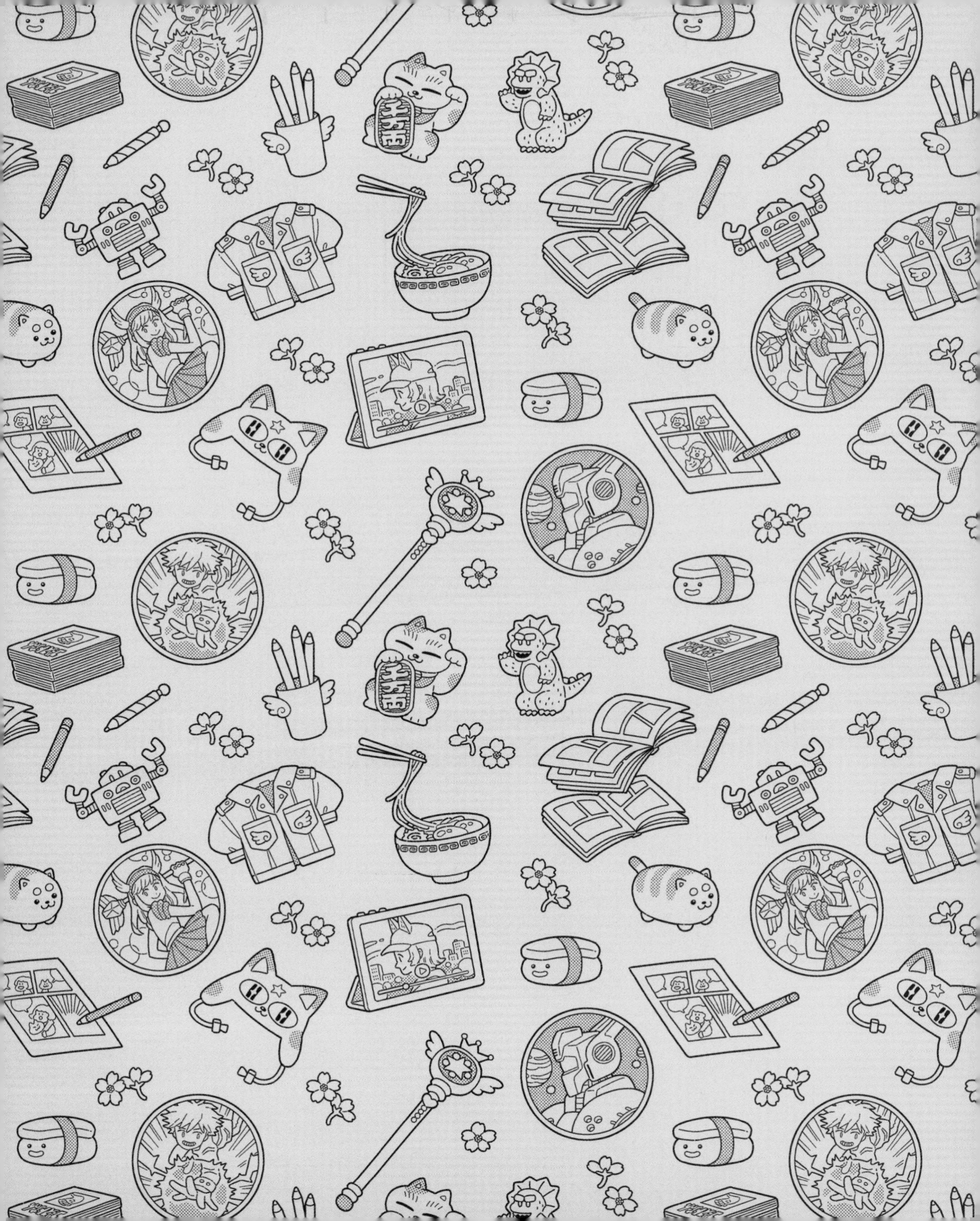

CONCLUSION

So THERE YOU HAVE IT! Our introductory guide to anime and manga.

Keep in mind that although we're at the book's conclusion, this isn't the end of your journey of exploring, watching, reading, creating, or sharing your love of anime and manga. Our goal with this book is to open the door a little wider to the exciting world of anime and manga, so that you can have a look around and see what excites you the most. But the more you read and watch and engage with anime and manga, the more you'll discover just how big these mediums are and how many doors are just waiting to be opened. The best thing about anime and manga is that there really is something for everyone.

Now, take your newfound knowledge and plunge right in! There's so much to be discovered, and you've only just begun . . .

"Believe in yourself and nothing can stop you."
—SAILOR VENUS

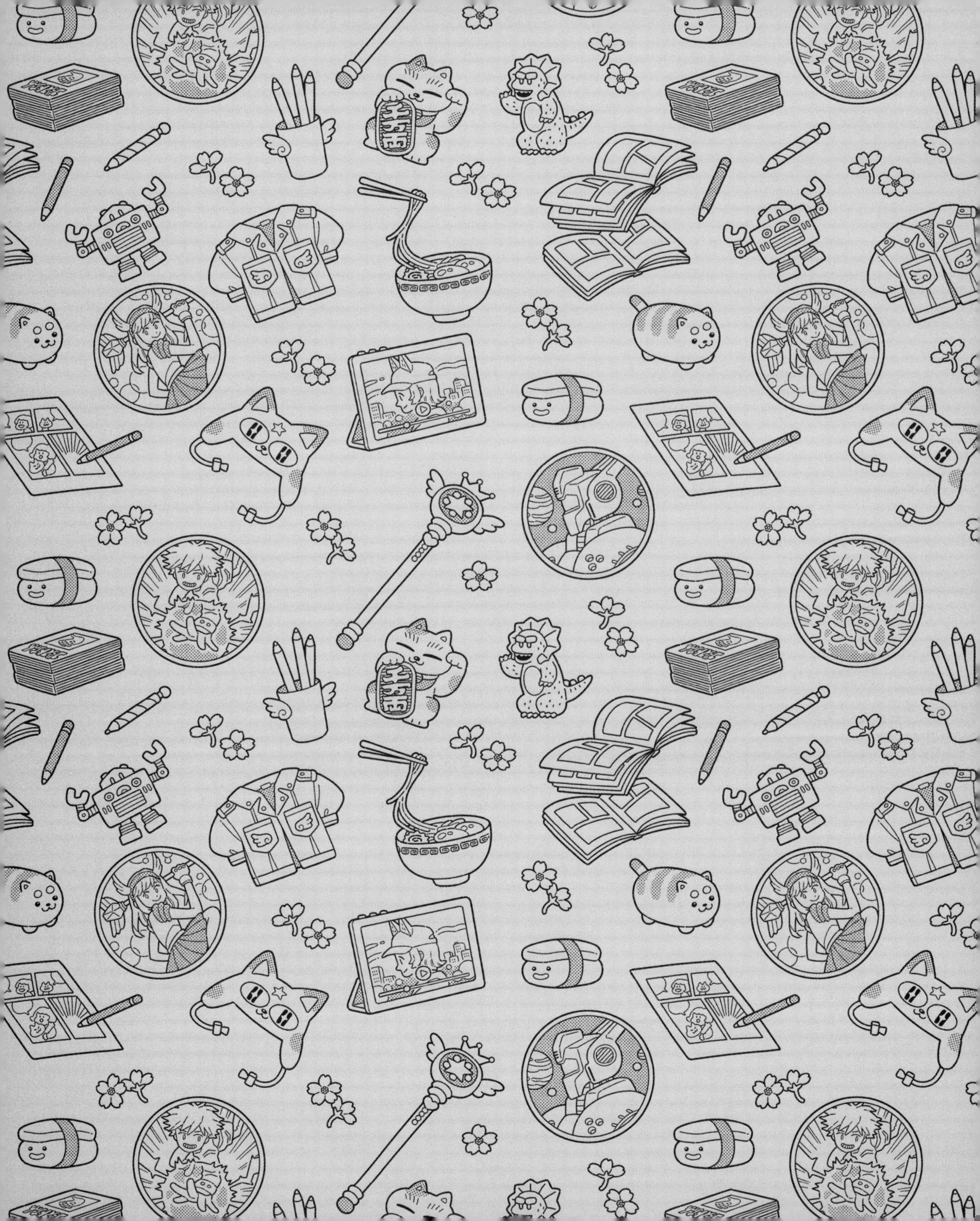

GLOSSARY

Anime: a deliberate Japanese shortening of the English word *animation*, anime is used to define Japanese animation meant for various age groups and demographics.

AMVs: short for anime music videos, these are common in anime fan culture and either have very talented or popular musicians compose the music for them or fans themselves edit anime footage to their favorite songs.

Cels: transparent plastic sheets of celluloid that contain images created by artists. Some animation cels have since made it to the collectors' market as nowadays most anime is created using computers with artists making their drawings on digital tablets.

Commissions: individualized illustrations/sketches made by artists for manga or anime fans in exchange for a fee. Depending on the artist involved, the fee can be costly, so fans will save in order to get a piece of art from an illustrator or animator they admire. Some cosplayers also take commissions to make costumes for paying clients.

Con Crud: a familiar name for colds that people bring home from conventions. After being surrounded by so many people at one time, it's no wonder a lot of people come away with the sniffles.

Convention: a place where fans can gather in large groups to see, meet, or interact with artists, writers, directors, producers, actors, cosplayers, and other pop culture industry professionals. Conventions are typically held at large event spaces over the span of two to five days.

Cosplay: a combination of the words *costume* and *play*, cosplay describes performance art where people create elaborate costumes and fashion accessories to represent characters from popular stories. (Though less common, sometimes cosplay can involve original characters as well.)

Doujinshi: self-published fan-made manga and small magazines similar to those you can find in the United States. These manga are often focused on fan fiction using characters from other popular manga and anime or sometimes from original works.

Dubbing: the process of using new scripts and voice actors to replace the original Japanese audio in an anime; also called *dubs*.

Fandom: a community of people who are fans of a particular character, story, person, or medium. Sometimes the word *fandom* is used to refer to fan communities as a collective whole.

Fukidashi: commonly known in English as a speech balloon, these shapes in manga are used to facilitate dialogue between characters.

Gunpla: a Japanese word shortened from *Gundam plastic model* that describes Gundam model kits, or the process of building mecha models for fun. Some people even elaborately paint their models and enter them in competitions.

Isekai: meaning "another world" or "a different world" in Japanese, this describes a hugely popular concept in anime. Influenced by video games, isekai stories typically involve characters that get sucked into larger digital universes and occupy game-tailored roles.

Josei: Japanese for "woman," in anime this means stories focusing on romance for adults (ages eighteen and older).

Karaoke: a Japanese invention where people sing along to their favorite songs using pre-recorded music and microphones.

Katakana: one part of the Japanese writing system, mostly used for the transcription of non-Japanese words into Japanese.

Kodomomuke: a wide-reaching genre of manga geared toward kids.

Kohai: a Japanese word meaning "junior" or "underclassman" often used by more senior members of society or organizations to refer to younger people or mentees. Kohai are meant to be mentored by upperclassmen, or *sempai*.

Manga: a word that means "whimsical pictures" in Japanese, manga is simply another word for comics—a narrative medium defined by sequential images placed in a deliberate order to tell stories.

Mangaka: a person who creates manga. The *ka* in *mangaka* denotes expertise, demonstrating that the person is a professional of the art form.

Mecha: a deliberate Japanese shortening of the English word *mechanism*. Mecha is the term for a science fiction subgenre that focuses on giant robots, or mechs.

Nemu: The katakana word rendition of the word *name*, nemu are rough drawings created as a road map for later drawing manga. In English, these are often called "roughs" or "thumbnails."

Otaku: a Japanese word that has come to mean a hard-core, obsessive fan or enthusiast. For example, someone can be a train otaku, an airplane otaku, and most certainly an anime otaku! Sometimes, people from outside Japan will call themselves otaku to let others know that they are fans of anime or Japanese pop culture in general.

OVA: short for original video animation, meaning an anime that went direct to video first instead of to TV or movie theaters.

Seinen: a Japanese word for "youth," in anime this means stories geared to a younger male audience (typically eighteen to thirty years old).

Sempai: a Japanese word meaning "upperclassman," used to describe someone who is an older member of society or an organization, whose job it is to mentor underclassmen, or *kohai*.

Sensei: an honorific or additional title often attached to the name of a mangaka. A sensei is usually a teacher or master, and the word can also be used to designate professors or doctors.

Shojo: the Japanese word for "young girl." Shojo anime refers to titles made specifically with a female audience in mind. Some of the most popular anime of all time have been shojo titles, including *Sailor Moon*, *Cardcaptor Sakura*, and *Ouran High School Host Club*. Shojo anime and manga often focus on friendship, romance, and relationships . . . but not always!

Shonen: the Japanese word for "young boys," this has also come to mean a certain style of anime, often springing from the pages of manga magazines like *Shonen Jump*. *JoJo's Bizarre Adventure*, *Demon Slayer*, and *Jujutsu Kaisen* are all good examples of shonen series that began as manga before becoming huge anime hits.

Slice of Life: a genre of manga that shies away from wildly dramatic plot twists in favor of focusing on characters living their daily lives, doing cute and/or heartwarming things, and making friends.

Sports Manga: a genre that involves all things sports. It's not limited purely to athleticism, however; sports manga can also include competitive activities like chess and card games.

Subtitling: refers to leaving the original voice performances in an anime in the original Japanese language, but adding readable text on-screen; also called *subs*.

Tankōbon: while this often means an independent or stand-alone book, the word typically is used to refer to manga volumes.

VIZ Media: an American manga publisher founded in 1986, and one of the country's largest and oldest anime publishers and distributors. Owned by Japanese entertainment companies, it continues to account for the largest share of anime and manga being introduced to U.S. readers today.

Voice Acting: a kind of performance in which actors provide voices for characters in animated films/series, audio dramas, and more.

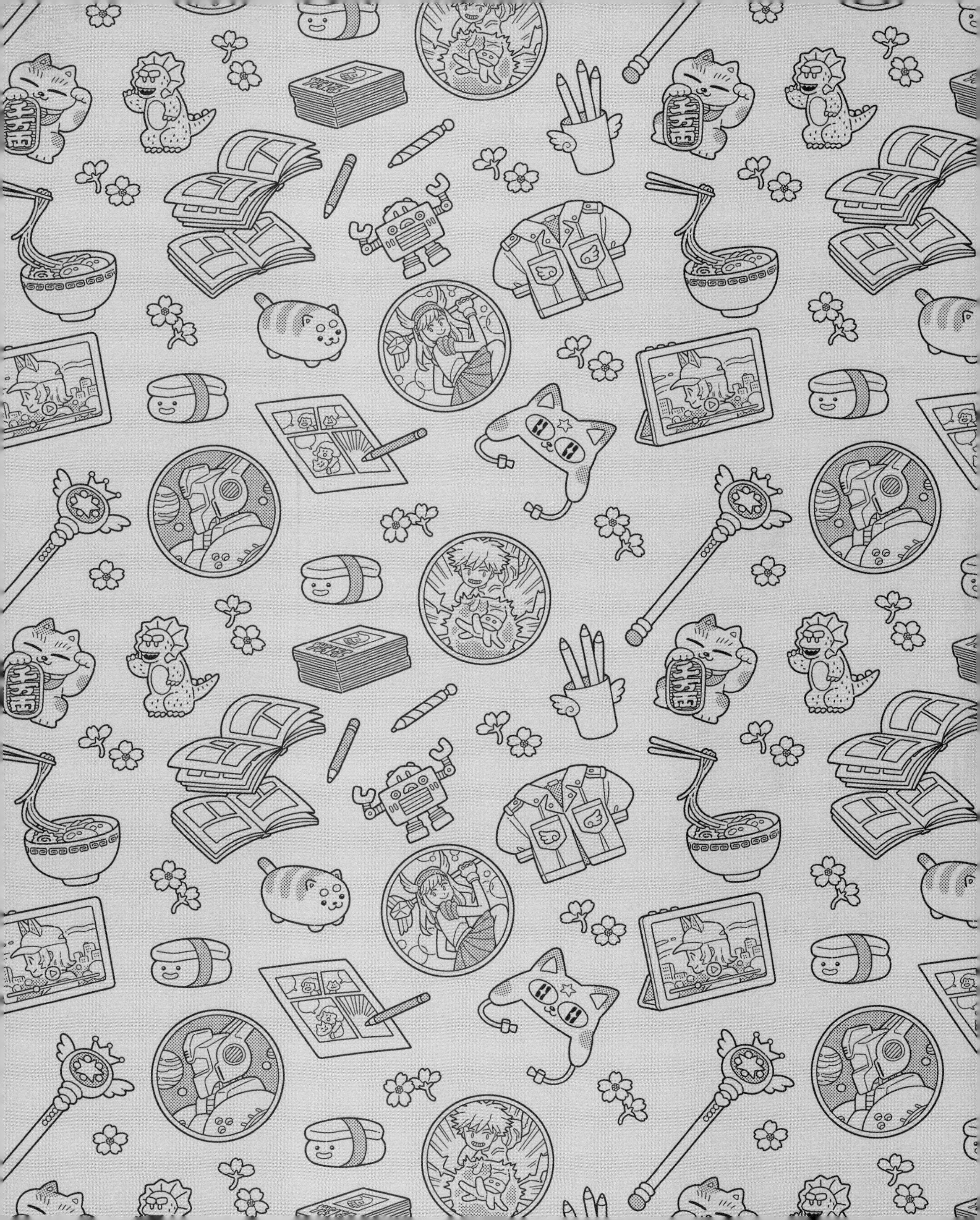

FURTHER READING

MOST OF THESE TITLES ARE written for an adult reader, but with your parents' permission, you may want to check them out to learn even more about the history, creation, and fandom around manga and anime.

The Art of Osamu Tezuka: God of Manga by Helen McCarthy

The Astro Boy Essays: Osamu Tezuka, Mighty Atom, and the Manga/Anime Revolution by Frederik L. Schodt

Manga by Nicole Rousmaniere and Matsuba Ryoko

Manga: Sixty Years of Japanese Comics by Paul Gravett

Manga: The Pre-History of Japanese Comics by Nobuyoshi Hamada

Manga in Theory and Practice by Hideaki Anno

Manga! Manga! The World of Japanese Comics by Frederik L. Schodt

Miyazakiworld: A Life in Art by Susan Napier

One Thousand Years of Manga by Brigitte Koyama-Richard

Pure Invention: How Japan's Pop Culture Conquered the World by Matt Alt

Starting Point 1979–1996 by Hayao Miyazaki

Turning Point 1997–2008 by Hayao Miyazaki

Watching Anime, Reading Manga: 25 Years of Essays and Reviews by Fred Patten

ACKNOWLEDGMENTS

FROM SAMUEL SATTIN

A book like this takes a lot of collaboration and creativity. First and foremost, I'd like to thank my cowriter, colleague, and friend, Patrick Macias, for embarking on this project with me and sharing his vast knowledge on all things manga and anime. Secondly, I'd like to thank our editor, Britny Brooks-Perilli, who brought this book to us and nudged it along into what it is today. I'd like to thank editor Julie Matysik, who helped bring this book across the finish line while Britny was out on leave. And of course, no acknowledgments section would be complete without a massive thank you to Dara Hyde, superagent extraordinaire. I'd also like to thank multiple other friends, colleagues, and loved ones, including Gary Sattin, Deb Aoki, David Hyde, Kara Dennison, Aki Yanagi, Jocelyne Allen, Kamome Shirahama, Dawn H., Deneen Melody, Vince Shortino, and Kate Hawk—a constant source of inspiration.

FROM PATRICK MACIAS

Thanks to my awesome coauthor Samuel Sattin, Utomaru the super artist, my superagent Dara Hyde, and amazing editors Britny Brooks-Perilli and Julie Matysik for making this book possible! Also, thanks to Julia Macias, Izumi Evers, Vincent Shortino, Matt Alt, and the staff and writers of *Otaku USA Magazine* for always keeping me sane and entertained!

FROM UTOMARU

Dedicated to all of my favorite anime and manga characters.

ABOUT THE CREATORS

SAMUEL SATTIN IS A WRITER and coffee addict. In May of 2022, he launched a Kickstarter with the artist team Gurihiru for Unico: Awakening in coordination with Tezuka Productions in Japan. He is also the writer of *Buzzing*, and the forthcoming history of roleplaying games, *Side Quest*. He adapted the Academy Award–nominated Cartoon Saloon *Irish Folklore Trilogy* (*WolfWalkers*, *Song of the Sea*, and *The Secret of Kells*) to graphic novel format, has written screenplays for PBS, and previously wrote books such as *Bezkamp*, *Legend*, and *The Silent End*. His nonfiction work has appeared or been featured in The Nib, *The Atlantic*, NPR, and elsewhere. He graduated with an MFA in comics from California College of the Arts and a creative writing MFA from Mills College, freelances in animation development, and works as a studio writer for Schulz Creative Associates, aka Snoopy Central. He currently resides in Northern California.

A LIFELONG FAN OF ANIME AND manga, **Patrick Macias** is the editor in chief of *Otaku USA Magazine*, the founding editor of Crunchyroll News, and the author of numerous books about Japanese pop culture, including *TokyoScope: The Japanese Cult Film Companion*. He also wrote the original story for the anime series *URAHARA*, which was streamed globally by Crunchyroll. Born and raised in Sacramento, California, he now lives in Tokyo, Japan.

U TOMARU IS A FREELANCE ILLUSTRATOR, art director, and graphic designer based in Tokyo, Japan. She studied graphic design at Tama Art University, where she developed her art style: bold line art, vivid colors, and dynamic composition. Her main influences are cartoons by Fleischer Studio, movie posters from the 1960s to the 1980s, and American and Japanese comics and animations. She is the author of *Kitty Sweet Tooth* and *Kitty Sweet Tooth Makes a Movie*.

IT IS DANGEROUS TO GO ALONE, HERE TAKE THIS!